HOW TO MAKE YOUR SALON WORK,

SO <u>YOU</u> DON'T HAVE TO!

Kelly Shaw

HOW TO MAKE YOUR SALON WORK,
SO YOU DON'T HAVE TO!

Copyright © 2021 by Kelly Shaw

ISBN 978-1-913713-28-7

First published in Great Britain in 2021 by Compass-Publishing.
www.compass-publishing.com

This publication is designed to provide accurate and authoritative information for the owners of Beauty Salons.

It is sold under the express understanding any decisions or actions you take as a result of reading this book must be based on your commercial judgement and will be at your sole risk.

The author will not be held responsible for the consequences of any actions and/or decisions taken as a result of any information given or recommendations made.

If legal, tax, accounting or other expert assistance is required you should seek the services of a competent professional.

Dedication

I dedicate this book to my perfect partner in life, my husband Amii. Thank you for all of your love, support and encouragement. For being my champion and not letting me procrastinate when things got tough. I couldn't have done this without you.

Contents

Foreword

Thirty years ago, I qualified as a 'Beauty Therapist'. I have always disliked the word beauty when used to describe our profession as it feels marginalising and trivialises what we do. I joined this industry because I was passionate about helping people to achieve skin confidence: through education, skin treatments and products underpinned with science.

I loved my training but, and it is a big BUT, I was told on numerous occasions that I would never make money in beauty! I felt disillusioned and was uncertain that I had chosen the right career. Yes, I loved the industry, but I also wanted independent financial security. Then out of the blue, a representative from a skin care brand called dermalogica came into college and literally changed my world. Talking retail sales and profit margins, cash flow and success, I found my people.

Now the Director of Education for dermalogica, I see that the salon industry puts more women into business than any other. They are part of a community of micro-entrepreneurs. High street CEO's who are job creators contributing billions to the economy through their uniquely powerful human touch.

Like Kelly, I have always championed the respect and success of the professional skin therapist and yet still we see independent salons fail. Not for a lack of incredible treatments and empathic touch but for a lack of confidence in business acumen. There is a lot to be said for the early days of opening your own business when you are brave and naïve, and anything is possible. But for any business to grow, employ a team and thrive, it's not enough to just offer amazing treatments. You need a powerful business tool kit that is practiced by every staff member and continually evolved.

In this fantastic guide you will have numerous 'AHA' moments. Simple formulas that have the potential to help you create not only a financially successful business, but a happy and thriving team. It has never been more important to understand your 'why'. This is a time for elevating and amplifying your reason for being. But it will not happen by chance or because you alone believe in it. It will require your whole team to be with you in your purpose and in your success.

I have been fortunate to work with Kelly both as a colleague and as a salon owner. With many years of experience in the industry as a successful business owner and true entrepreneur, I can think of no one better than Kelly to share her best practices.

I recommend that you open your mind and bring your fully authentic and perfectly flawed self to these excellent principles. After all, if you are not on stage with the team, you are a bystander in the audience.

Sally Penford – Director of Education for dermalogica

Chapter 1

It's all about YOU!

If you're reading this book, then I'll make an educated guess that *'something isn't quite right with your salon'.*

You could be experiencing anything from a **little frustration with your staff**, to a **full-blown fear** about whether you can keep the doors open.

It's possible you're questioning your motivation because you're living with the constant feeling of ... **it's too hard,** or this is 'NOT' what I signed up for when I opened.

You may even be wondering ... **why didn't anyone warn me it was going to be like this!**

The truth is many salon owners don't want to admit that their reality is a far cry from their original dream.

Why do they feel the need to hide the truth?

Because in this social media driven world, where everyone has the **'perfect salon'** we don't want it to look like ours isn't ... *do we?*

So what's the reality for most salon owners?

- Some of us **give up.**

- Some of us **hope for the best** but gradually fall more and more out of love with our business each year.

- A surprising number of us **read** books like this one, looking to make things better, but never actually **'DO'** anything consistent and constructive with what we learn.

I say **'US'** because, like you, I'm a salon owner and before I discovered and applied what I'm going to share with you in this book I went through *ALL* the stages I've described above.

I fell out of love with my salon. I had **struggles with my staff,** I wasn't **making as much money** as I'd expected. I felt like a hamster on a wheel, **doing the same things but expecting different results** and this is the key point ... I was blaming everyone or everything else for what was happening.

- I can't find **'good staff'** ... that's the problem.

- It's a **'tough economy'** so clients aren't spending ... that's the problem.

- It's the **'new salon'** that just opened down the road ... that's the problem.

Challenges like these, which appear to be out of my control, have to be the problem ... don't they?

Unfortunately, the answer to that question is ... **NO!**

They often look and feel like it, but that's an illusion. Instead they are just the *symptoms* of the real problem.

I didn't discover the difference between the symptoms and the real causes of my problems until sometime after I reached my ... 'SOD IT' moment and decided ... **"enough is enough, I'm not giving up and I'm not carrying on like this either ... something has got to change."**

Reaching your 'sod it' moment can be very powerful, but it's a power that has to be focussed towards learning the right lessons and acting on them.

Now you might not want to hear this next bit but here goes: The **first lesson** I had to learn and take action on was that ... my biggest problem was **ME**.

This means ... and I know it can be tough to hear ... if you want things to get better in your salon, you're going to have to realise and accept, LIKE I DID, that your biggest problem is ... **YOU!"**

I would understand if, right now, you're rolling your eyes, swearing and thinking, *"what a load of c**p Kelly, why on earth would I be causing these issues when all I want is for my staff to be happy, serve lots of clients and be part of a successful salon?"*

If you are, I'd like you to take a deep breath ... hold it for a count of five and then slowly let it out.

Hopefully you're now feeling a bit more relaxed and when you're ready to move on I'd like you to turn your attention away from any indignation you may have been feeling about being told that you are the problem and instead answer this simple question.

Do you have staff problems like I used to?

- Do you struggle to find **'good'** staff?

- Do you struggle to keep **'good'** staff?

- Do you struggle to motivate **your** staff?

Like you may well be doing now, I used to think problems like these were the fault of my staff, but as I mentioned a few moments ago, they were only symptoms of the real problem.

Once I learned how to interpret the symptoms, a bit like a doctor does, I understood they were telling me that either:

- I was hiring the **wrong** people because I wasn't recruiting properly, or

- I was attracting the **right** people but not giving them the employment experience they expected or were promised when they joined me, because I wasn't leading or managing them properly!

I learned that if you don't get your recruiting, leadership, or management processes right, it **inevitably** leads to staff leaving to find something better, or causing problems because they want things to change, or even worse they end up sitting back and doing the minimum they feel they can get away with.

This means if **YOU** want **YOUR** staff problems to disappear, **YOU** are going to have to look at **YOURSELF** and how **YOU** recruit and lead/manage **YOUR** staff.

Now, the blunt truth is that you recruit the way you do at the moment, because you **'believe'** that's how you should do it. You lead and manage the way you do, because you **'believe'** that's how you should do it.

Change your beliefs about what is possible and how things should be and your behaviour will change to match ... it's automatic, just like night follows day.

When I came to the realisation that the cause of my problems were my limiting beliefs, plus the negative emotions and emotional insecurity that came with them, I took stock, looked at the facts rather than my feelings and realised I'd taken my eye off the salon.

My personal life had taken priority and everyone at the salon had been left to their own devices, with **no vision** or **structure** to follow. I'd assumed that everything would carry on as normal because they were all lovely people. They would instinctively know what I'd want and exactly how to do it.

When I look back at this now I think ... *"I must have been crazy, how on earth had I expected that strategy to work?"*

So let's look at you for a minute ... and I mean **really** look. It's a very difficult thing to do and most salon owners won't, but if you really want to **see a change** in your business you're going to have to **become the change** you want to see.

Do that consistently and others will follow you.

We'll talk more about getting people to follow you later in the book, but for now let's simply understand that at the moment you are inadvertently causing your own problems!

You're probably only doing this because of some subconscious beliefs you developed as a child.

Yes you're now an adult, with life experience and a fully formed character but what you probably don't realise is that when you feel threatened or insecure it's the underlying beliefs of your childhood emotional needs that drive your behaviour.

For example, before I understood what was really happening I **'believed'** I should have a **hugely successful** salon that would **work without me** needing to be there.

After all, I knew what I was doing and had lots of experience ... so why wouldn't it?

My experience came from working my way up to a senior corporate management position whilst travelling the world working with **prestigious** brands such as **Four Seasons** and **Shangri-La Hotels**. Working with them to build, open and run world-class Spas.

Yet here I was, 7 years after opening my own salon and I still wasn't happy.

Don't get me wrong, mine was a great salon and we were successful; we had won awards and had become an integral part of our community, but it wasn't giving me the life I wanted.

I knew something wasn't right so I'd read all the books, blogs, articles, and online courses about running salons, anything I thought I could learn from ... and I did learn but most of the time I just **didn't use** what I'd learnt because I'd unknowingly become a **world class procrastinator!**

It was after attending **another** conference (*because maybe the answer was there?*) that I came into contact with a business coach who worked with salon owners. As we chatted I began to **see things differently** and knew I needed to change.

It wasn't easy and I didn't do it by myself and I'm not even sure I'd have succeeded if I had tried to do it without my coach to guide me. It's for that reason that I'd highly recommend you find someone to help guide you through this process of self-discovery if you can.

The first thing I discovered came as a bit of a shock because I have always thought of myself as a confident person with high self-esteem.

Imagine my surprise then, when I understood that I was actually holding myself back subconsciously because of a **FEAR.**

It was my **fear** of losing good staff who *I was afraid I wouldn't be able to replace.* It stopped me from being assertive when I needed to be. It meant I wasn't clear and consistent in communicating my needs and the needs of the business. I compensated by trying to **please everyone** and **this** was the underlying cause of my staff problems.

The limiting belief of not being able to find good replacement staff triggered a feeling of fear that subconsciously drove the behaviour that was sabotaging my salon ... **but the good news is, once I had the facts and understood what was happening, I learnt how to manage it.**

Please understand my fear hasn't gone away completely, it's just that it doesn't control my actions anymore. For example I'd be lying if I said I hadn't experienced any fear while I've been writing this book. I've caught myself thinking, *"what if no one reads it, or what if it isn't any good?"*

When those thoughts pop up now, **I have the tools to see them for what they are, so they don't stop me from achieving my goals anymore.**

The tools I've just mentioned are now part of a whole suite of tools I created with my coach, that have transformed my experience of running my salon … and now I want to share them all with you.

That's the purpose of this book.

We're going to begin the process by helping you to see yourself differently because as I discovered … **who you think you are and who you really are can be quite different!**

So let's get started and we'll begin with the basics.

We all have a self-image and it consists of three things:

1. How we see ourselves (our self-esteem)

2. How others see us

3. How we **believe** others see us

The most powerful of the three is **how we see ourselves**, and it's important to understand that our **self-image** may or may not be an accurate picture of who we really are as a person. We **believe** it's true and even **behave** like it's true but it may not be, **it depends on how healthy our self-image is.**

I *believed* I had a very **positive** self-image. I *believed* in myself and that I could **achieve anything** I set my mind to. I mean I'd opened countless **successful spas** and I had opened and built a **successful salon** hadn't I?

I couldn't have done all that without a **positive** self-image, could I?

What I didn't see was that there was something else going on inside my head, an unconscious script I didn't even know was there, that kept interrupting and planting seeds of doubt.

It wasn't even anything major but just enough to keep me **stagnating** instead of **driving** towards the success I knew I could achieve. I had an emotional insecurity that was holding me back and although it wasn't there all of the time, its effects were enough to stop me moving forward.

Could that be happening to you as well? You'll know for sure in a moment.

Take a look at the following questions and with each one choose the number between 1 and 10 that reflects how strongly you feel... with 1 meaning **DEFINITELY NOT** and 10 meaning **DEFINITELY.**

These are very important questions so take your time and think about your answers carefully and honestly.

* **Are you afraid of making mistakes?**

Definitely Not   1 2 3 4 5 6 7 8 9 10 Definitely

* Do you find it hard to say no?

Definitely Not 1 2 3 4 5 6 7 8 9 10 Definitely

* Do you try to be perfect?

Definitely Not 1 2 3 4 5 6 7 8 9 10 Definitely

* Do you expect perfection in others?

Definitely Not 1 2 3 4 5 6 7 8 9 10 Definitely

* Do you often feel guilty?

Definitely Not 1 2 3 4 5 6 7 8 9 10 Definitely

* Do other people let you down a lot?

Definitely Not 1 2 3 4 5 6 7 8 9 10 Definitely

* Do you find it hard to trust?

Definitely Not 1 2 3 4 5 6 7 8 9 10 Definitely

* Do you put other people on a pedestal and think they're better than you?

Definitely Not 1 2 3 4 5 6 7 8 9 10 Definitely

* **Do you worry about the future?**

Definitely Not 1 2 3 4 5 6 7 8 9 10 Definitely

* **Are you a born sceptic?**

Definitely Not 1 2 3 4 5 6 7 8 9 10 Definitely

How did you get on?

If you scored four out of ten or higher on any question, this is a clear sign of emotional insecurity and low self-esteem ... *even if, like me, you haven't been aware of it up until now.*

Remember, if you're serious about **making your salon work, so you don't have to**, you need to do something about this or you'll **never** get where you want to go.

Why?

Because *insecurity is like an emotional disease;* it's often hidden but it sucks the positive emotion out of a salon by eating away at confidence, trust and your ability to connect to other people in a healthy way. **Take trust, confidence and connection away from a salon and it will never enjoy long-term consistent success.**

Fact: Dig away at any business that's either stagnating or constantly struggling with problems and you'll always find an owner who's fighting a battle with insecurity and a poor self-image.

If you want more evidence you've been affected, ask yourself how many of the following are true about your salon.

Do you find:

- Nothing gets done unless you nag?

- It's easier to do things yourself?

- Your staff room atmosphere can be bitchy?

- It's hard to confront **'difficult'** people?

- You keep losing staff?

- You find it hard to trust some of your staff?

- You put off price increases because you don't want to lose clients or deal with moans from your staff?

- Your salon struggles to grow?

- You can be moody or stressed at work?

If you answered yes to even **one** of these questions, then you have even more evidence you need to deal with any insecurity and strengthen your self-image as a matter of urgency.

Put it off, as many of you will, and you'll find the ideas and tools I'm going to share with you simply won't work.

You might be wondering how insecurity and a poor self-image can be so damaging?

Well, try thinking of your self-image like the operating software of a computer. When it's working properly, your computer can do fantastic things. When it isn't, **nothing** works the way it should and you find yourself wasting time, getting frustrated and going round in circles.

Your self-image controls **your** operating software, which is made up of:

- Your emotions.

- Your beliefs.

- Your behaviour patterns.

Your emotions can be positive or negative, and we all live with a mixture of both, but in the same way a computer has a **'safe'** mode to revert to when things go wrong, your subconscious mind has a **'safe'** emotional response to fall back on when you're under pressure!

Let me show you how damaging it is for our **'safe'** emotions to be negative; starting with a list of the most common negative emotions:

- Anger

- Fear

- Guilt

- Sadness

- Hurt

We all know people who get 'angry':

- They blow up for the slightest reason.

- They're often bullies. We respond to them differently depending on the state of our own self image. We either choose to confront them, avoid them completely, or walk on eggshells if we 'have' to deal with them!

We all know people who are ruled by 'fear':

- They can be indecisive, hard to motivate and absolutely **hate** confrontation.

- They may be frightened of failure or getting things wrong, **so they don't take risks.**

- They may be frightened of success, so **they sabotage anything that starts to go well because they think they don't deserve it.**

- They may be frightened of looking silly, being seen as cocky or standing out from the crowd.

- They may be afraid people won't like them, so they try to 'please' everyone.

We all know people who are driven by 'guilt':

- They feel **'guilty'** about not **'doing'** enough or not being **'good'** enough, no matter what they do.

- Their guilt drives them to be impossible to help, or please, or even worse they can be unreasonable perfectionists. No matter **what** you do for them it's never enough or good enough, is it!

We all know people who are 'sad':

- They're the glass half empty people who tend to notice and dwell on the negative news and incidents that happen to us all at different times in our lives.

- They see setbacks and tragedies as confirmation of their view of the problems and sadness of the world.

We all know people who wallow in 'hurt':

- They tend to be life's **'victims'**.

- They focus obsessively on the people and events they feel have damaged them, or robbed them. They use these events to feed and justify their behaviour.

- To them, the reasons for their problems are always outside of themselves; when things go wrong it's **never** their fault, they've always got an excuse!

We all see and know people like these don't we? What most of us don't realise is how often other people look at **us and see the same sort of behaviour!**

Salon owners with any of these traits will find they attract staff problems like flies around s**t, and that can easily undermine your ability to effectively recruit, lead, manage, and motivate people.

Your salon will not thrive if you can't do these things well, will it? The good news is there is a simple answer, but before we look at it there's an **important point** I need to make.

Having a poor self-image doesn't mean you're stupid or make you a 'bad' person; it's just a reflection of how your unconscious mind is wired up at the moment. **The good news is, we can change how we feel about ourselves.**

I mentioned earlier that **limiting beliefs** hold us back as well and you'll see that they nearly always go hand in hand with **negative emotions.**

When I started to look at myself, I could see examples of these **negative emotions** which I'd never noticed before, it was like this is just what I do, a sort of auto-pilot. I found that when I was **'under pressure'** something happened that made my operating software revert back to **'safe'** mode and these negative emotions suddenly took control. *And because it was happening subconsciously I just went with it and believed it was real.*

For me **'safe' mode is FEAR** and it's not a nice place to live and one that I could never understand because I'd taken tremendous risks in my career.

I'd moved halfway across the world in my 20's to live in Thailand, to manage one of the top 10 Spa's in the world at the time, The Four Seasons Resort, having never even set foot in a spa before in my life.

I wasn't scared then, so why now having my own salon was I petrified that I might get it wrong and lose the business?

I'd managed teams of over 50 staff so why was I now bending over backwards trying to please all my staff in case they weren't happy and didn't stay?

It just didn't make sense to me; logically I knew the doom and gloom scenarios that constantly played in my head were silly but they felt so **real.**

Here's a quick question that will help you see the link between a poor self-image, negative emotions and limiting beliefs.

Do you think people who are driven by anger, fear, guilt, sadness or hurt would **'believe'** it's:

- OK to trust?

- OK to let go?

- OK to delegate?

- OK to look for possibilities in every situation?

- OK to fail from time to time; mistakes are simply lessons to be learnt from?

NO!

I know I certainly didn't believe them, and because I didn't believe them it made it **impossible** for me to actually do any of them.

How was my salon ever going to fulfil my needs for it to work without me being there if I couldn't do any of these things?!

Eventually I understood that successful leaders and managers **DO** believe in them and **would DO** them, but the really important point is that I **now believe them and I have done them.**

I truly believe that I can help **YOU** believe them too as long as you're prepared to work on your self-image and self-esteem.

The good news is there are lots of powerful tools to choose from and you'll need to find the one(s) that work best for you **... and then use them consistently.**

As a guide for you, I tried **meditation** - *which I thought would be weird but I love it and still do it daily,* **reading books** *(the right ones this time, which I would discuss with my coach and then implement what I learnt where it was appropriate!)* and if you like quick results and you don't mind paying for them you could try **Rapid Transformational Therapy (RTT).**

My coach was a huge fan of Paul McKenna and used his hypnosis programmes to effectively overcome his own insecurities. Paul's book with accompanying CD called *Change Your Life In 7 Days* (which is available from Amazon if you want to give it a try), was also very beneficial to me in helping me change my mindset and limiting beliefs.

Now if this chapter has opened your eyes to what's going on, my advice is to jump straight in and start tackling this yourself first using any one of the tools I've just mentioned.

However, if the thought of working through it on your own is a bit daunting, I'd love to help. If that sounds like something you'd like to explore please contact me, and we can talk it through ... you'll find my details at the end of the book.

In the meantime just remember, once I started to **see things differently** and understand how my thoughts sub-consciously **impacted my actions**, which would then impact on my **salon performance**, things began to change.

I'd taken the first step and I hope you have the courage to reach out and take yours as well.

Chapter 2

Take Responsibility

The blunt truth is ... for better or worse you and your business are wherever you are right now and there's no point in beating yourself up or looking back at what could have or should have been.

Instead, begin the personal development work that chapter one proved you might need to do and then move on by **taking responsibility** for your future.

It's not always going to be easy and there will be times when you want to give up, *I know I did*, but I **promise you** it will be worth it at the end.

Remember, you can do your 'chapter one' work while you're developing your vision, systems, processes, and standards for your salon.

I actually found it beneficial to work on both my business and myself at the same time because the two definitely affect each other, so if you're ready to make a start ... **let's jump straight in**.

I want you to begin by considering **'<u>why</u>'** you're in business.

Is it just a means to an end and a way of paying your bills or ... are you passionate about creating a business with a sense of purpose that stands out from the crowd because it makes a real difference in people's lives?

I'm asking because most of the salon owners I have met simply **'fell into'** salon ownership.

We either got offered the chance to own a salon or found ourselves working for people who didn't appreciate what we did and decided we'd be happier or earn more if we worked for ourselves.

Surprisingly, few salon owners have a *'life dream'* to open their own salon. Those that do, tend to know exactly **what** they want to achieve and **why** clients will be attracted to it.

If you just fell into salon owning and it's just become a means of paying your bills and all you're looking for is some advice that makes some of your pain go away ... **I can tell you now this book isn't going to help you much!**

Why not?

Simply because you and your goals lack passion and purpose and you're going to need passion and a sense of purpose if you're going to take responsibility and it matters because ... **if you don't take responsibility, you're abdicating your role as leader of your business.**

A business with no leader exists in a vacuum that your clients and staff will inevitably try to fill by getting their own personal needs met as a priority.

This leads to a bunch of individuals all pulling in different directions, while your business at best goes nowhere and at worse ... **goes BUST!**

You'll have noticed that I've used the term *leader* and not manager. Have you ever wondered what the difference is?

I've asked many salon owners this question and very few have known, in fact many didn't think there was a difference.

This is an expensive mistake because the difference between them is huge and one of them is far more important than the other **if you want your salon to work, so you don't have to!**

A *leader* has passion and purpose. A *leader* creates a vision, they paint a picture of what they see is possible and then **inspire** their team and **engage** them emotionally so they are happy to work together to turn the *leader's* vision into a **reality.**

A *manager* is focused on getting the current job done, **supervising** people or tasks and working on **specific** goals or targets to meet **deadlines.**

Now both of these roles are important for your salon to be successful but your role as **salon owner** should be that of the *leader.*

It is your responsibility to lead your salon and team to success; **how well are you executing that at the moment?**

Do you have a vision, a big picture of how your salon should be?

Have you shared this vision with your team and are they on board working with you every day to help you achieve it?

Leadership is the **key** to you having the salon/life you want to achieve.

When I took responsibility for my part in where my salon was going and started to lead my team ... **amazing things began to happen.**

As the leader of your salon your job is to provide your team with the **skills** and **resources** needed to do their jobs. To create an **environment** where it is easy for them to take responsibility for their decisions and actions.

You will need to be **firm** and **courageous** and understand it's inevitable that sometimes your actions will cause **conflict** ... when it happens you just need to be **confident!**

Remember, confidence comes much more easily once you recognise your limiting beliefs, which is why you need to keep working on yourself as well as your salon.

To give you some context for all this, when I first opened my salon I'd just moved back to the UK following my international leadership and management roles in the spa industry.

As much as I loved all of the spas with their great locations and amazing facilities, I never really connected with the guests because they were transient holiday makers who weren't there for long.

Yes I met some nice people and some returned year after year ... **but it wasn't the same as working in a salon.**

My vision for the business was simple.

To consistently provide a 'salon' visit that came with extra touches that made the whole experience extra special and 'spa' like.

This worked well and our clients loved it.

We began to notice that because of our **customer service** and how we *treated* our clients they became **loyal fans** and **recommended** others to us.

In the beginning I was very hands on and the salon grew consistently for years, but life never stands still and there came a time when I wanted to step back and devote more time to my personal life.

I thought I'd got it all planned but it didn't take long after I'd stepped away before our consistency and standards began to slip and the recommendations began to dry up.

It takes a while but this change was reflected in our trading figures and I had to work out what was going wrong. In the end I had to accept that the salon only really worked when **I was the one driving it.**

It was *me* at reception greeting clients, making them feel special and making those **connections** so that they truly felt part of our business.

Don't get me wrong, my team were good and lovely people, but together we hadn't created an environment where everyone **knew** what was expected and the standards or rules we all needed to work towards.

This was down to my lack of understanding about what leadership required. It was all very well that I had a vision and I had shared it ... **but it wasn't written down.**

I also hadn't created any standards for <u>how</u> things needed to be done, nor had I set up systems to measure whether the standards I should have set were being delivered consistently.

Worse than that, I had no system for holding anyone to account either!

How could I expect things to run how I wanted them to if nobody knew what was expected or was held accountable?

No wonder things started to fall apart. I blamed everybody and everything but myself and unfortunately this led to some great members of the team **moving on.**

I felt insecure, betrayed and let down and, surprise, surprise ... my negative emotions and the **limiting beliefs** that underpinned them, started to take a hold.

As I've shared in the previous chapter, once I made this realisation with the help of my coach ... I **took responsibility.** Responsibility for redesigning my salon so it worked just how I wanted it to ... **whether I was there or not!**

That is when I started the process of literally making myself redundant. Now I'm not saying this is the right step for every owner, but the journey I went on and the steps I have put in place can be adapted for any business.

It may be that you **love your treatments** and would prefer to spend time in a **treatment room** rather than trying to do clients and fit in **managing** your staff. The process I went through can **help** you to achieve this.

It may be that you are **working alone** but want to *grow* and take on a member of staff; this process will help you get it right from the start.

Or you may already have a salon with staff but you **constantly have struggles** and don't know how to make things run smoother and more effectively so that you can achieve your goals and dreams. The process I went through can help you with that too.

The journey we will go on together now is the process I went through to achieve a salon that makes my team, my clients and me happy.

I am going to share **tips** and **tools** to help you do the same; it doesn't mean your vision has to be the same as mine. These are **fundamental tips** that can help *any* salon, and I know from experience of working with salon owners just like you that putting these steps in place will **help the majority** of salon owners **reach their goals.**

You may not necessarily do them in the same order as me, your business will dictate what your priorities are and how you should implement the tools I'm going to give you.

If you're ready, then join me in the next chapter where we look at the subject that most salon owners struggle with ... **motivating their team!**

Chapter 3

Your Team

Let's start at my beginning!

My salon clearly didn't run the way I wanted it to when I wasn't there, yet for me to be happy this is what I needed it to do.

Now that I had the tools to manage my negative emotions I was excited about getting stuck in!

We had been in limbo for a couple of years and as we celebrated the salons next anniversary I took some time to reflect. We'd lost a few key members of the team and I'd gone ahead and recruited replacements, which in hindsight was not the best plan (more on that later!).

It was **back to basics;** I had to look at my team and really assess if they were the **right team** to be able to get me to my goal.

What did I need from them in order to be able to achieve my vision?

- I needed someone who wanted to be **part of a team.** Someone whose **values** *aligned* with mine. Someone who was prepared to be part of a team that was happy taking responsibility and would **work with me** to achieve my vision.

Instinctively I knew that **not everyone within my current team** fitted into these parameters, and there were some that could **sabotage** my vision.

I realised I needed a **process** for recruiting and working with my team. My coach had a tried and tested formula which inspired me to adapt and develop one for my own situation and I still use it in my salon today.

It has been adapted for the salon owners I coach too and now I'd like to share the structure with you.

Let's begin with the word **TEAM**. The acronym ...

Together

Everyone

Achieves

More

...is often trotted out by trainers to explain what makes a team work but I realised I needed to take this further if I was going to have a team that could fulfil my vision. I realised I needed my team to be **'emotionally invested'** in the salon, each other and me.

This is where I discovered the concept of **'Team Esteem'** which is defined as:

"A group of individuals who unite around a common belief or idea and feel good about working constructively together to further that belief or idea."

It's like emotional glue that sticks a team together, allowing them to feel safe and secure, supporting each other as well as the salon.

This is exactly what I wanted but I couldn't just go ahead and impose **'Team Esteem'** it had to happen naturally. I needed to create the right environment and have the right people so that it would happen automatically.

The first rule I learnt about building **'Team Esteem'**, was **No Hyacinths!**

If you're wondering what a Hyacinth is, that was my first question too when I was introduced to this concept … let me explain.

Hyacinth Bucket was a character in a popular TV series in the 90's called *Keeping Up Appearances*.

Now Hyacinth wasn't a bad person, she's just a brilliant example of a square peg trying to fit into a round hole. She is desperate for the world to see her in a certain way so she can feel secure and happy; the problem is, in trying to make **herself** comfortable she damages the environment for **everyone** else.

If you've seen the show you'll know exactly what I mean but if you haven't then just go to YouTube and type Hyacinth Bucket into the search box and see her in action!

When you've got the picture just ask yourself:

- In meeting her needs … does she make her husband happy or does she make his life hell?

- In meeting her needs… does she make her neighbours happy or make their life hell?

It's pretty obvious isn't it; she makes life hell for just about anyone she comes into contact with!

What does this have to do with our emotional glue I can hear you ask?

Well, there may be people within **your team** who are perfectly nice people, but in getting *their* emotional needs met (whatever they may be) they make it difficult for others to work together and if that isn't happening, the glue won't set and you won't build **'Team Esteem'.**

Now, if like me, you are starting to get the point about the damage Hyacinths can unconsciously cause, your next question is going to be.... **how do I know if I have any?**

Here's a simple exercise that will help you identify them. To complete it you'll need a piece of paper and a pen.

When you're ready, make a list of all of the names of everyone you employ or who's involved in any way with helping you run your salon.

This includes parents' partners and spouse if you have regular contact with them, because they can all have a profound effect on your ability to run your salon!

When you've done that, take each name on your list in turn, and based on your experience of working (or living) with them, ask yourself the following four questions.... *(Go with your gut reaction when you're doing this exercise and take no more than 5 seconds to answer any of the questions)*

Question 1

Does this person have an attitude I'm comfortable with, and the skills to do the job I want?

YES or NO

Question 2

Does this person have an attitude I'm comfortable with, but their skills need improving to get to the right level?

YES or NO

Question 3

Does this person have an attitude I find frustrating and challenging but has the skills needed to do the job well?

YES or NO

Question 4

Does this person have an attitude I find frustrating and challenging, and do their skills need improving to get to the right level?

YES or NO

Each time you ask this series of questions, the person concerned should end up with **3 'No's' and 1 'Yes'** and all I want you to do is make a note of the **number** of the question you answered 'Yes' to, next to their name on the list.

Is that what you've got? Great, now what do we do with this information?

Ask yourself, who deserves your time, energy, support and encouragement?

- The people who are supporting you and have an attitude you can work with?

  Or

- The people who frustrate you, and want to pull you in different directions to suit their own agenda?

The answer is obvious isn't it? You work with those that want to work with you and they're the people who've got a number 1 or number 2 next to their name. The 3s and 4s are your Hyacinths!

When I sat down and did this exercise I had a team of 8 and a mixture of all of the numbers. Even just sitting and doing this simple exercise started to get me thinking about certain individuals within my team and I didn't even know what to do with the information I just received.

Like some of you have probably just discovered, I had quite a few 3's. Therapists who were great with clients, always booked and made the most money. I would excuse their behaviour because I was scared of losing them or I didn't want to upset them. I would spend my time trying to motivate them, thinking of new ways I could engage them, incentives, prizes and team buildings.

My goodness it's exhausting just thinking about it! I did exactly what I shouldn't have and spent so much time trying to turn around my Hyacinths that I forgot my 1's and 2's. The people who I did enjoy working with and supported me and each other.

I let them get frustrated too and, in some cases, leave because I was focusing on the wrong people.

This seems crazy to me now and I know some of you will be doing just as I did and experiencing those same situations. It was like a light bulb moment for me and I knew that if I was going to make my salon work ... **my Hyacinths had to go!**

So instead of trying to bribe or motivate my Hyacinths into changing their behaviour I learnt to do just 2 things:

1. Every time they break a rule or cause a problem, take them to one side and in a quiet, non-emotional, professional manner, tell them what they've done wrong, explain it's unacceptable and be very clear what the consequences will be if they do it again.

   Most importantly you can't wimp out of delivering those consequences if they do cross that line!

2. Every time they do something positive that you want to encourage, **pay them the compliment of noticing and say well done.**

The rest of the time don't try to '**motivate**' or '**change**' them anymore, simply <u>ignore</u> the dramas and just interact with them in the day to day need of being polite and working together.

It's a little strange at first but the more you stick to it the easier it becomes. This will only work though if you have a positive self-image and high self-esteem. You will find that if you stick with it consistently one of two things will happen.

1. They'll get fed up because their tactics aren't working anymore and leave.

2. They'll modify their behaviour to get more of the praise they now deserve and you won't want them to leave.

Either way your team and your salon just got a whole lot better!

I was a bit sceptical about this process when my coach first shared it with me; if I'm being honest it seemed too simple and I didn't think it would work.

However, when I put it into practice changes began to happen really quickly and the good news is … I got exactly the results I was promised.

In other words, the team members I had issues with either left of their own accord or adapted and became engaged with me and the rest of the team, enabling my goals to be reached.

So let's assume your anti Hyacinth process has done the trick and your 3s and 4s have gone … **what do you need to do to get the best out of your number 1s and 2s?**

The first thing I had to do was simple enough … **but it did make me aware that I didn't really praise my team enough when they did a good job; I just expected them to know.**

By consciously being aware and making the effort to praise everyone when deserved I saw a shift in how the team responded to me ... **a very positive one!**

The second thing was a little trickier for me. I puzzled over how I could determine when they've broken a rule or caused a problem, when most of the time it's not that obvious?

It made me realise that in order for me to carry this out and for it to work, we needed to have **specific rules or systems** in place so that I had something to back me up. If there isn't a system in place how could I tell someone they weren't following it?!

Cue the light bulb over my head again and the realisation that we needed to have systems in place in order for this to work.

It was also the next logical step for me in achieving my goal, because if we had systems in place for everything we did, I wouldn't need to be in the salon to make sure everything was done the way I wanted ... **the systems would do it for me!**

It meant we needed to get organised and although we already had a procedures manual, it wasn't that in-depth and nobody ever really followed it.

The main reason for that was because there weren't any **'consequences'** if they didn't!

I realised that meant I needed **comprehensive systems** in place that worked and were **consistently delivered** by my team and myself.

Anyone that couldn't or wouldn't deliver in future could be efficiently dealt with by the **'Hyacinth'** system which allowed me to comfortably explain the issues and consequences.

I also realised I couldn't just impose a whole new set of systems and expect my team to take ownership. Instead they had to be involved in creating them.

By the way, getting your team involved in creating your rules, systems and processes is a great way of spotting any Hyacinths you may have missed … **so you can weed them out before they do any more damage to your business!**

So let's assume you've now got a Hyacinth free team, how can you make sure you don't hire any more in the future?

You just have to read and implement what you learn in chapter 5, but before you do that we'll look at how you need to work with your existing team!

Chapter 4

'This Is How We Do Stuff!'

The title of this chapter is our 'user friendly' name for systems.

Systems need a user-friendly title because the word itself sounds techy and boring, but hopefully by now you've realised that systems are actually going to become the **'fundamental structure'** of your salon in the future.

If you don't have them in place **and** being used consistently to the point where they become your team's culture, you'll never be able to take your salon to a place that makes you happy.

When my coach first started talking about systems, I was confident I understood what he meant, after all I'd written countless operating manuals for Spas during my time as a Spa Consultant and Director of Spa.

I even had an operations manual for my salon so I was adamant I understood, until I was questioned about how well they were implemented. At that point I realised I didn't really have an operations manual at all ... **instead I had a big dusty folder no one ever took any notice of!**

I realised how **powerful** processes and systems could be if they were done properly and became the **'culture'** of the salon.

It sounds so simple but this was another real light bulb moment for me. I understood that because I'd been doing them wrong for over 20 years I'd never fully understood **'their power'**.

I also realised that creating them now was going to be much easier than I thought, because a lot of what was happening in the salon was actually already working, and **already** part of the culture ... **it had just never been written down and seen for what it was.**

My coach's instructions were brief and to the point!

*"Get your staff to start writing down what they do. Tell them it's all going in our new **'This is how we do stuff'** book, so that when anyone new joins in future they can be given the book to read so they can learn how we do things here!*

*While your staff are doing this ... **you spend your time making a list of the things that are not working as well as you'd like at the moment.**"*

This was of course the simple way of putting it and I'll share how I actually implemented the process in a moment but before I do I want you to think back to the concept of **'Team Esteem'** I told you about earlier.

I realised I needed to implement this new process in a way that made my team feel **secure** and that their involvement in creating the salon systems and culture was a **crucial** part of helping them feel secure and would soon lead to the consistent day to day operation of the salon ... **and because it would become second nature to them they'd need very little policing!**

In order for it to work, we would have to set aside a regular time each week for us all to get together to discuss our progress. I decided that I would allocate 30mins each week to solely focus on systemising the salon rules that were already working and to work together to improve or totally re-invent those that weren't.

IMPORTANT POINT!

By the way these meetings never stop happening because **change is a constant in every business**, whether you like it or not, so your rules, systems and processes will **always** need reviewing and refining.

At the beginning of this process I'll admit I was a little apprehensive about introducing the idea to the team ... **cue limiting beliefs and negative emotions!**

However, now that I was starting to recognise them for what they were, it was becoming easier for me to acknowledge the feeling but then dismiss it. **Especially in this case because I could sense this new way of working with my team was going to be a game changer for my salon.**

To introduce the concept of our **'This Is How We Do Stuff'** manual to the team I decided to talk about the problems I'd seen them getting stressed about becasue we didn't have consistent procedures in place. I told them I'd come up with a way of making that stress and those problems disappear and asked if they wanted to hear about it.

They said yes!! So I explained ...

- That because things weren't **standardised** at the moment it was hard for them to know what was **expected** of them and it was hard for me to praise or discipline them for what they **were** doing as well.

- That the lack of consistent positive feedback for the good stuff they did, or consistent censure for the not so good stuff, was eroding trust and confidence.

- That we were going to standardise everything together, we'd approve what was working and tackle together the things that weren't.

- How this would make things **fairer** for everyone.

They really warmed up to the idea that it was a way for us to decide as a 'team' how to do things and that once we'd agreed a procedure, we would all then sign it to say we understood it and would stick to it.

Just take a moment and read that paragraph again to fully understand and appreciate the power of having these systems, processes, and procedures, in fact whatever you want to call them, in place in **your** salon.

You'd have a set of **procedures** that your whole team have **agreed** to work by and a document signed by all of them to say they understand, and this was agreed by everyone.

Think what this would mean when it comes to doing your one to one's with the team; the recognition you can give them for following standards. The areas they excel and you can show praise for going above the standards agreed to.

However, also think what this would mean if you ever got into a situation where you needed to go down a disciplinary route … you'd have your evidence of non-compliance right there.

This also makes recognition fair for 'above the normal' performance and helps manage any unacceptable performance or behaviour of your team members a much easier task!

When we first started having our meetings I wanted to make sure it was a positive experience, so the first subject I chose was something that was really bugging them.

For us at the time we were having an issue with clients being late which meant therapists were getting stressed because of the unnecessary pressure it put on the rest of their day when they were fully booked.

Dealing with this problem together turned out to be the perfect way to begin creating the first procedure for our manual … **This is how we deal with late clients.**

Uncertain at first because this was a new concept for all of them, they soon began to take an interest when they realised this was something that affected them personally.

Splitting them into pairs, we outlined the problems we needed to solve. Each pair was then asked to go away and discuss it for 5 minutes and be prepared to share their thoughts, feelings and ideas with everyone else.

When they came back I had a whiteboard and pen ready and asked them to tell me what frustrates them.

Within minutes I had a page of negative responses of how this made them feel.

Therapists complained how sometimes reception just expected them to squeeze in additional treatments without considering how it impacts their day.

Reception said they felt uneasy when they had to tell a therapist that clients were late because they'd become very negative towards them.

It was also noted that clients are often impacted by this negativity.

After everyone aired their grievances, things started to change, they recognised their behaviour and how this might impact the clients' experience.

Ideas about how we could accommodate late clients in other ways started to emerge. By the end of the session we had a complete **This is how we treat late clients procedure** which not only included the practical rules but also set standards for what the *attitude* of the team should be.

In fact it was so successful that they even came up with a slogan for how the team should respond to this situation in future *"Anything I can do to help?"*

This applies to the client but also each other as a team, how can they support their colleagues.

This was exactly what I had hoped would happen … and then something I didn't expect to happen, happened.

The team started to suggest ideas as to what we needed to look at in our next meeting, so we agreed it made sense to carry on solving the urgent problems as our first priority.

We chose problems like, *'This Is How ...*

> *... we keep the salon clean.'*

> *... we manage tint tests.'*

> *... we deal with staff lateness.'*

Once we had worked through all the urgent issues together, we naturally progressed to procedures that actually helped to **create our salon culture**, *'This Is How...*

> *... we provide the client journey.'*

> *... we work as a team.'*

> *... we deal with complaints.'*

> *... we retail our products and services.'*

As each procedure was finished, we would put it in place and monitor it for a period of time to make sure it worked.

If it didn't we would discuss and tweak it so that it did.

The great thing was how issues in the salon stopped being **'people problems'** to me, instead I saw them as **'system problems.'**

If a problem did come up it was the system I looked at first not the **individual.**

If it turned out that the majority of the team were following the procedure with no problem and in fact it was a people problem ... the problem person was dealt with using a system ... the *Hyacinth* system I shared with you earlier.

Just take a moment to think about it...

We now had a set of rules we had all signed and agreed so if someone was not following the rules, I had something to back me up.

I was able to take the team member aside and explain calmly they weren't following the procedure we agreed, and what the consequences would be if this continued.

It made it easier for me to be more **assertive** with my team as the situation wasn't **confrontational.**

It was simply based on facts that couldn't be argued with.

The results were exactly what were promised when I was introduced to the *Hyacinth* system.

Either the person left because they weren't getting the results they wanted anymore or their behaviour changed and they became an integral part of the team.

Yes it took time and it wasn't an easy journey but it has resulted in creating a team that has real **'Team Esteem'** and fully supports each other, the salon and me.

You must be prepared for things to change as you go through this; it might sound shocking but of the 8 original team members I had when I began this process only 2 stayed in the long term. (The others left for their own personal reasons). Yes the others going was the realisation of one of my biggest fears ... **but the reality was far less traumatic and ultimately even welcomed.**

I knew that to get my salon where I wanted it, I needed a team who **'believed'** in what I was trying to achieve and **'wanted'** to be a part of it.

It meant that as we brought new people on board to replace those who'd gone their own way, we could make sure they had the same values as us and wanted to be a part of what we had created.

I hope you are starting to realise the power of having these systems in place and the power they have to give you the salon of your dreams.

If you still need convincing about the power of systems used properly then I suggest reading the book *The E Myth Revisited* by Michael E Gerber.

When I read this book I was already working through our systems so it felt great to confirm I was on the right path!

Let's move on now and remind ourselves that we agreed in chapter 1 that your salon is a reflection of you and your current beliefs and that if you wanted a different experience you needed to change your current beliefs.

Creating our 'This is how we do stuff' book really helped me with this.

Remember I was still working on my self-confidence and self-esteem at the same time and found having the systems really helped me to understand and detach from my low self-esteem and this gave me the confidence to become the impartial referee of our salon rules.

I was able to deal with red card situations without taking them personally.

I was able to shut down ideas and behaviour that didn't suit me or the business, but doing it in a positive constructive way, giving them reasons why it was a definite no. This wouldn't be possible if you couldn't detach from a low self-image.

Can you see how all this fits together now? I really hope so because it's how I thrived as I went from an original team of 8 down to 2.

In the next chapter we will look at how to recruit the right replacements.

Chapter 5

Recruiting The 'Right' Team

If you've read this far, you'll know why this chapter is so important and if we're being honest every salon owner who's been in business for more than a few months has made mistakes when it comes to hiring, so if you know you have ... you're not alone!

For me, I believe one of the main reasons for this was because I was usually **'desperate'** to find someone.

I believed there was such a shortage of **'great'** therapists and then when I came across one, I would make them fit into what I was looking for, although in hindsight most of the time I never really knew what I was looking for!

As you know the *Hyacinth* system was effective in moving on the staff who could have held my business back; now another system, my recruiting system came into play in making sure those that left were replaced by the right people.

If this had happened previously, I would have done what I always did (panic a little) and advertise everywhere to try and find more therapists.

Then I'd interview whoever had the most experience and came across well. If they seemed OK I'd get them started a.s.a.p. ... **clients were waiting!**

Now I know better, let me share this knowledge with you, so you don't make the same mistake.

The first thing I had to approach in a different way was my job advert.

Up until then, like most of you I'm sure, I had always just placed an advert (whether online or print) that stated the job vacancy, qualifications/experience required and a general description of the package being offered.

I was then introduced to the marketing concept called **A.I.D.A.** and explained how it could be applied to a job advert to attract the right candidates for my salon.

At first I thought it was bonkers and that I wasn't brave enough to write an ad in this way, but I pushed through my **FEAR** *(I was getting good at that!)* and thought ... *what have I got to lose?*

What I've been doing hasn't worked so why not give it a go ...

So I did!

A.I.D.A. is an acronym that's designed to lead you through the steps you need to follow to attract the right candidate's attention and then lead up to the point where they apply for the job.

The letters stand for

1. **Attention**

   Attract your ideal candidate's attention with a powerful headline. *A great headline is 80% of the secret of a successful advert. You only read the article in a newspaper or online that grabs your attention... It's the same with adverts!*

2. **Interest**

   Now you've got their attention, you need to build their interest in the job you're offering.

3. **Desire**

   There's a difference between being interested in your job and really wanting to work for you... NOW! This is the step where you make that happen.

4. **Action**

   Finally ... Now they really want it ... Tell them **exactly** what they have to do to get it.

IMPORTANT POINT!

Before you start writing your advert you need to be clear about exactly <u>who</u> you want to apply for the job, **what** they're missing at the moment and <u>why</u> you're the employer who can give it to them!

Now that's explained ... let's start with the headline and the secret is to make the headline about *them*, or *their problem*, not about *you*, or *yours.*

If your headline says ... **"Therapist Required"** or **"k:SPA Are Looking For An Experienced Therapist"**, it's about you, isn't it?

If however your headline says ...

"Are You An Experienced Beauty Therapist Who's Fed Up With Having To Work On Saturdays/Weekends In A Negative Atmosphere Where You Feel Underappreciated?"

It's about **them** and is far more likely to get their attention!

By the way, research has shown that putting your headline in **"Quotation Marks"** and starting each word with a **Capital Letter** will increase the response to your advert, so it's a good habit to get in to!

Now let's build their interest.

How? ... Tell them a story!

Tell them a story that paints a picture and stirs up feelings that go with your **'imagined'** version of their current situation. While you're doing it you can add yourself to the picture and explain **'why'** it would be different working for you.

Let me give you an example. If your imagined **'perfect candidate'** was an experienced therapist with a strong following who's been attracted by the *"Fed Up With Having To Work On Saturdays/Weekends In A Negative Atmosphere Where You Feel Underappreciated?"* headline you could say ...

"If you are then I know how you feel because I, like you, felt frustrated working every weekend, missing out on time with my family and feeling I was being taken for granted.

When I started my own business I made a promise to myself that I'd never make the same mistakes with the therapists I employ, and if you read on you can hear from two of them who've been with me for several years, how well I've managed to keep that promise."

Using the A.I.D.A. approach you've now got their attention and generated interest; you've explained why it would be different working with you. You can even continue the story by showing them how you've delivered on the promise by using quotes from existing members of your team about what it's like working for you.

"I think k:SPA is a great salon to work in because it's got such a friendly and welcoming atmosphere, and not just for clients but for all the staff as well. As a therapist I am always given new opportunities and goals to work towards.

We work extremely hard as a team, this ensures k:SPA is kept running to the best standard possible. We always perform treatments and complete tasks to the highest standard. Although none of this would be possible without Kelly and her way of running k:SPA."

Ashleigh - Senior Therapist

"k:SPA is a warm and welcoming salon, Kelly is always looking to progress her staff to the highest level to ensure our clients receive top quality treatments and service from her team.

Kelly is a good motivator and encourages her team constantly keeping it an exciting place to work. The friendly atmosphere between staff and clients make it a pleasure to work at k:SPA. The team here all have a lovely relationship and always look forward to our next team night out!"

Taylor – Senior Therapist

You could include images of your team happily working in the salon or enjoying themselves on team nights out. There's a lot you can include, isn't there, just remember to make the experience of being a member of your team come alive.

You can also include an idea of **'on target earnings'**, staff training and any other perks that come with the bonus of working for you.

"Well paid with generous on target earnings. We are committed to on-going training and development, which is why what we're offering is not just a job but a career packed full of opportunities should you desire them. Most important of all you will be part of the team where you will be heard and treated with respect".

When you've painted the picture you can move on to **Desire** ... the desire to take action and contact you **NOW**. The secret to this is ... scarcity. Scarcity of time or scarcity of availability. Both approaches work well to give people the push they need to act and you can introduce them in a couple of ways.

1. With a deadline ... *"applications have to be in by etc, etc."*

2. With a high demand ... *"last time we advertised we got nearly 30 applicants, so it makes sense to call now and get in early."*

The final part of your advert is **Action**. Never assume what they have to do next is obvious. **You have to spell it out word for word for them!**

> *"Pick up the phone and call me between 3pm and 5pm on Monday 1st June ..... for a brief introductory chat."*

By the way, my personal preference is to screen applicants briefly on the phone, rather than asking for a CV or application form.

Why?

Because, I believe it's the cheapest and fastest way to sift out the time wasters and get to the people who might fit your team.

The fact is that talking to someone will tell you a lot more about what they are really like, than reading a form they've filled in – *or should I say someone 'might' have filled in for them* - because research has shown that 40% of application forms and CVs sent in contain ... shall we say ... **'factual inaccuracies'** and even the truthful bits will have important facts left out and a positive gloss put on everything!

If you haven't already guessed, the examples I've given you for your job advert are taken from an advert I did to find new members for my team. Although I had doubts about the process I can promise you it worked so much better than the box standard adverts I'd used before!

Now let's assume you've got some worthwhile **'applicants'** and move on to the selection process. We need to be careful **'who'** we employ, because:

- Not everyone will prove to be trustworthy.

- Not everyone has the ability to do the job you want them to do.

- Not everyone will have an attitude you're comfortable working with.

So how do you create a selection process that helps you find these things out sooner rather than later?

- You do it by building a clear picture of the self-image, beliefs, values and attitude of the person you're thinking of employing, *as quickly as possible.*

- You do it by not relying on **your** judgement alone. *You get the people they are going to be working with involved in the decision as well.*

- You do it by not just relying on an interview and trade test to make your final decision. *Your selection process should have several steps and take 3 months in total.*

Now I agree that in our industry a 3-month selection process might seem like an awful long time but getting value for the money you spend on wages is so important.

Did you know that employing the wrong person could cost you thousands because of lost time and clients and also damage to team morale?

Can you afford to be that sloppy in your hiring decisions? I know I can't! Wouldn't it better to be professional and take a little more time and trouble over it?

Of course it would, but sadly most salon owners don't.

Instead they think *"I know I should do it properly, but I don't know how and anyway I'm busy at the moment ... I'll do it next time"* and sadly for them ... next time never comes. Instead they carry on making the same mistakes again and again, while wondering *"why does this always happen to me?"*

So, we're agreed. It's important to have a selection process to help us identify the right people to employ and the good news is, I'm in the middle of sharing one with you!

- It's a process that gives your applicants reliable information about working with you and your team; they've got a decision to make as well, haven't they? *If the truth about your salon is so unattractive that it would put an applicant off if you spilled the beans, you'd better sort that out before you recruit anyone else!*

- It's a process that makes it almost impossible for candidates to avoid revealing their true **'self'** to you.

Before I get into more detail about the **'process'** ... here are four guiding principles to follow:

1. **Conduct your selection process in the 'right' frame of mind:** *It's so important not to be desperate. A saying I was once told that has become a sort of mantra is: "It's better to have no staff than the wrong staff."*

2. **Hire slowly and fire quickly**: Take the time to interview candidates thoroughly, then give your team the chance to meet them and express an opinion as well, before you finally decide to offer a 3 month trial period or not *and if you have any doubts or concerns during those first 3 months, take that as a sign, let them go and be prepared to start again.*

3. **Don't take anything you're told at face value:** *Use it as a starting point for further discussion and that's it!*

4. **Know what you're looking for:** You must understand that getting a feeling for a candidate's self-image, attitudes, beliefs and values is **far** more important to you than a picture of their current skill level.

Follow these principles and you won't go far wrong. Now let's move onto the detail I promised you:

- When you interview, choose a suitable venue that sets the right tone. Don't use your staffroom or anywhere that you can be interrupted.

- If you don't have a suitable place in your salon, use a local hotel or a coffee shop. I've found as long as you buy tea or coffee at regular intervals they're quite happy for you to be there.

- How and where you sit is important, so to help you get your body language right, sit at the same level as the person you're interviewing with no barriers between you and preferably at a 90-degree angle to them.

- Start the interview with a brief scene setting speech which makes lots of points that they would naturally agree with and *nod a couple of times every few seconds while you're saying it to promote agreement.*

- Remember, while we are interviewing, what you're **really** looking to discover are the beliefs, attitudes and values that make them **'who'** they are.

- The secret to doing this is by combining reflective listening with some simple questions. Learn to use these together and interviewing will become **very** easy for you!

We'll get to the questions in a moment, but remember, on their own, they **don't** have any special significance. You absolutely must combine them with reflective listening to make them work.

Here's a step by step guide to using reflective listening.

When you both sit down at the beginning of the interview ... *sit like they do.*

If they:

1. Fold their arms, *fold your arms;*

2. Cross their legs, *cross your legs.*

3. Sit upright, *sit upright yourself.*

4. Slouch, *slouch yourself.*

5. Lean towards you ... *lean towards them, and so on.*

Then for the first two minutes **'reflect'** any changes they make in how they sit. You take the time to do this because it makes them feel comfortable.

By the way, becoming a reflective listener is easy if you follow a simple rule, which is: 'don't think about what you're going to say next ... *just watch and listen carefully until they've finished talking!'*

Watch for:

1. A change of expression on their face: *they may smile, raise an eyebrow, blush or go pale.*

2. A change of posture: *they may sit back, sit forward, lean towards or lean away from you, cross or uncross their arms or legs.*

3. A gesture with their hands: *they may point at something imaginary, sit on their hands, make a chopping or pushing gesture. They may wave their hands about, touch their nose or mouth or scratch their head.*

All these changes can be a sign of a **'reaction'** and behind a reaction is an **'emotion'** and that's what you're after, because you're looking for what matters to **them.**

Now, once you spot it, you must reflect their **'reaction'** back at them, in a follow up question, to help you find out more about the **'emotion'** behind the reaction. Make sure you reflect the **same** word(s) and gesture(s) back to them when you ask your question.

For example, they might say ... *"I love making people feel good"* *(As they say it you see them smiling and nodding their head)*

You could turn their reaction into a question like *"I can see you 'love making people feel good"* *(you smile and nod as you say it, just like they did)* and that's important in a job like this, isn't it. Tell me about the last time you made someone feel good. What did you do?

Can you see, you're repeating part of what they said, in the same way they said it, but you've used it to create a powerful question.

Remember, reflecting language and gestures back to anyone you talk to, will give them the feeling you understand them deeply. This means they are far more likely to open up and tell you more. In fact, when you learn to reflect well, **you'll get to know them much better than they really want you too!**

Don't forget you've got 2 eyes, 2 ears and only 1 mouth, so listen and watch very carefully while you're reflecting ... **at least twice as much as you talk!**

IMPORTANT POINT!

When I was first introduced to reflective listening and tried it for myself it felt very strange and uncomfortable. I was convinced the other person knew exactly what I was doing and would think I was mad! I can promise you; THEY WON'T HAVE A CLUE!

It's quite normal to feel this way but if you practice, practice, practice and get really comfortable using it ... your life and your salon will never be the same again!

I say 'life' as well as salon because like most people who get really comfortable with reflective listening, I practiced on family first.

The fact is, once you take the time to get comfortable using it, the power of reflective listening can improve your relationships and your ability to understand people and your personal life really does get better.

Now, let's get back to the interviewing process and before we get to the helpful questions I promised, I want to remind you that on their own they have no special power.

Combined with reflective listening they give you the power to become a brilliant interviewer.

IMPORTANT POINT!

If you find you're getting through the questions in less than half an hour it's a sign that you're not using reflective listening properly.

When I first started using these questions I got through them really quickly and didn't find they gave me much information apart from the obvious answers.

If this happens to you too, just practice until it becomes second nature and you'll find yourself talking less, listening more and asking better follow-up questions, without even thinking about it!

Now when I use these questions, I find I often can't even get through them all in the time I allow for an interview.

You'll find yourself having fun and feeling in control in a way that never happened before.

With that point understood, here are the questions.

1. *"If I was talking to your best friend and I asked them to describe you in 3 words or less, which words do you think they would choose?"*

2. *"I'd like you to take a look at these 4 shapes and tell me which is your favourite?"* ... **When they've told you, ask them for their second favourite and so on. I'll explain how you use their answers after we finish the questions.**

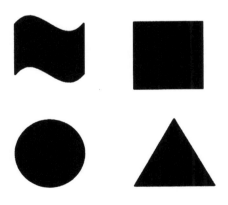

3. *"Sometimes we're inspired by people we know, sometimes it's someone we read or hear about. I'm interested to know who you think has been the most inspiring person in your life?"*

4. *"A recent survey showed that people in our industry enjoy their job more than any other profession; what do you feel makes it so enjoyable?"*

5. *"If I gave you £10,000 and said you had to spend it in the next 24hrs what would you do with it?"*

6. *"Everyone in our team needs to be comfortable taking responsibility so I'd like you to give me an example of something you've done that shows you're a responsible person."*

7. *"Where do you see yourself in 5 years time?"*

8. *"If money was no object; what would you do on your perfect holiday?"*

9. *"Tell me about the last time you felt really successful."*

10. *"Give me 3 reasons why I should seriously consider giving you this opportunity!"*

How do those questions feel to you? When I was first introduced to them I thought they were a bit strange, and had nothing to do with what I needed to get from an interview. I was wrong! Once I had practiced my reflective listening and used these questions, I learnt so much more from a potential candidate then I ever thought possible.

I was able to tell whether this person in front of me had the same belief structure as the team and myself. What was important to them and would we as a salon be able to fulfil their needs too.

I hope you can see how powerful these questions will be when you use them as revealing conversation starters. I know I can!

Now I promised to explain about the shapes, didn't I!

You'll find them very interesting, and they are one of my favourite questions for really getting people to open up, because the **'order'** the person choosing them comes up with suggests **a lot** to you about their priorities and what makes them tick.

People who choose the square normally:

- Love detail.

- Make lists.

- Hate being late.

- Always tidy up and put things away after they finish using them.

People who choose the circle normally:

- Love people.

- Enjoy entertaining them.

- Like caring for them.

- Only feel complete when they're in the company of other people.

People who choose the squiggle normally:

- Love change.

- Hate being tied down.

- Are always changing their minds.

- Are often late.

- Are disorganised and untidy.

- But they do come up with great ideas!

People who choose the triangle normally:

- Are driven to get things done.

- Get to the point.

- Are focused.

- Are competitive.

- Often don't care if they upset people.

I explain that most of us are a 'combination' of characteristics from 2 and sometimes 3 of the shapes; but we all have a dominant way of behaving.

I then explain what the order of their choice **'suggests'** to me about **them** ... and you'll be able to sense from their reaction whether what you've said is true or not. *(Do watch for their reaction carefully, because this exercise is only about 80% accurate so you won't be right all the time, but as you'll see in a minute ... it doesn't matter).*

You can really have fun with this, because right or wrong, you'll find you can build on their reaction by asking great follow up questions with your **reflective listening** abilities and when you do, you'll discover **more** about what really makes them tick!

Just remember it doesn't matter which way you get to know them better, *all that matters is you do get to know them better!*

Now, let's go back again to the selection process. If after you've had your 'reflective listening' chat you're pretty sure the person isn't who you're looking for, simply thank them for coming and tell them when and how you'll let them know about your decision.

If you do think they have potential, pay them the compliment of saying so, and then ask; *"What questions would you like to ask me?"*

As you answer their questions, look for the right time to give them a clear picture of what they can expect if they're successful. For example, I'm always looking for the right opportunity to say:

> *"You must understand that I'm not looking for just a therapist; I'm looking for an Ambassador. Someone who as well as performing treatments to the highest of standards, will take responsibility for all other aspects of running the salon, who will work as part of the team to support their colleagues to ensure the salon is successful.*
>
> *If you're successful and join us you'll be given the opportunity, tools and the environment to create a successful career, but, and it's a BIG BUT, whether you achieve it or not is up to you.*

Of course the team and I will be here to guide and support you, but we can't and won't do it for you; and if we ever get the feeling that you're not committed to making the most of every opportunity, we'll be parting company; now do you still want to join us?"

Do you know what?

If a candidate gets this far, they always say YES!

So ask yourself: *"What would my version of that speech sound like ... what do they 'really' need to know about working with us?"*

When you've finished your interview you then have to decide if they're good enough to go on to the next stage of your hiring process.

If they are, this is where you get your team involved.

Depending on what the applicant is currently doing you have to be flexible with this next step, I personally arrange for them to spend as much time as is practical with my team. It's normally a day or a couple of afternoons and I get them to spend as much time as possible with each member of the team.

I use the time for the team to carry out the trade test, not so much for skills but so they can talk to the applicant and get to know them. I also get the applicant to contribute whatever they can to the running of the salon including cleaning, laundry and room set up.

We then allocate some time for the most important part of the process ... **the getting to know you game.**

This can change each time so that it is new for the team as well as the applicant and is a great way to get to know each other in a fun environment.

One example of a game we've used for this required everyone to type *(so the team can't recognise each others handwriting!)* 3 obscure facts about themselves.

They all get put in a bowl and then we take turns picking one out and reading it to the group, everyone then writes down the name of the person they think this fact belongs to.

Then the fun begins, because as you each say the person you think, things get a little deeper. People try to justify their decision and when you finally get the person to admit who it belongs to even more information comes out!

It's a great way to see how the applicant interacts with the team and vice versa. You'll see if they are happy to give it a go even though they are on the back foot because they have no point of reference with anyone else.

By the way I encourage my team to choose the most random facts about themselves to make it fairer when guessing and it also means that as a team we discover even more about each other too!

At the end of our time together I ask every team member for their decision and if **any** of them say no, that's it ... the applicant goes no further. If they all say yes *(and normally they do if I've done my job at the interview properly)* then we offer the applicant a 3 month trial and they usually accept!

At the end of the 3 months as a final check I ask every team member for their final decision and again if anyone says no ... the applicant leaves.

Now the reality is, if there are any doubts or problems, they tend to surface much sooner than 3 months and if they do crop up I always investigate and try and solve the problem ... once! If it doesn't work I take it as a sign and the applicant leaves.

And that's it.

You've come to the end of a powerful, widely used, tried and tested recruitment process that can transform your salon.

We've been talking about recruiting the right people and recognising them in our own team, haven't we, so now I want to look at the other side of the coin which is creating the right environment.

Chapter 6

The 'Team Esteem' Staircase

Here's the process I use to create the right environment for my team to thrive in, and get that **'emotional glue'** we talked about in chapter 3. We need to learn how to lead our team members up 'The Team Esteem Staircase' and when you think about it logically the place to start is...

STEP 1 ... IT'S JUST A JOB.

If any of your team get stuck on Step 1 ... you'll know.

You'll know, because to them what they do **'is just a job'** which means they'll turn up, go through the motions and go home. **That's it.**

STEP 2 ... EMOTIONAL SECURITY.

This is where we add the 'emotional glue' that holds your **'Team Esteem'** together but be warned:

- It's the tough step.

- It's the danger zone.

- It's the step on **'The Team Esteem Staircase'**, most salon owners get wrong at one time or another, (including me!)

You'll find if you haven't got everything else we've talked about in place the chances of getting it wrong go through the roof … **and yet in theory it should be so easy!**

To get our emotional glue setting correctly we need to provide our team with, **an emotionally secure environment and we do that in 4 ways:**

1. By providing an emotionally attractive belief, idea or goal for the team to aim for or live up to.

2. By behaving in a way our team members can trust, respect and appreciate. *(These are all emotion-based words and we'll look at what they mean in a moment.)*

3. By only employing people whose contribution <u>we</u> can trust, respect and appreciate. *(In other words … NO HYACINTHS)*

4. By only employing people who can trust, respect and appreciate each other. *(It's those HYACINTHS again!)*

IMPORTANT POINT!

In many ways the words I've just written in the list on the previous page are the most important in this book because they are the key to creating a happy staff room, attracting value for money staff and loyal fan clients who don't complain and are happy to spend!

So, bearing that in mind I'd better say a bit more about them hadn't I!

1. "By providing an emotionally attractive ideal or goal for the team to aim for or live up to."

This uses the incredible power of **'Towards Motivation'** a vision you as the leader of your salon have created, shared with your team and are all working towards together.

A Hyacinth free team which feels emotionally secure will have high **'Team Esteem'** and a very positive **'team-image'** which means they'll be quite capable of making effective choices as a team and achieving positive goals.

2. "By behaving in a way our team members can trust, respect and appreciate."

This is really about any damaging bad habits you may have as an employer. When I was introduced to the concept of 'Team Esteem' one of the things I had to look at was my behaviour. You see I was causing a lot of my own staff problems and I didn't even realise it! I was given a set of questions to answer to see if I had any bad habits that made it impossible to build high team esteem.

Here are 13 questions you can ask yourself and answer honestly to discover whether any of your habits might be making it difficult for your team.

1. When you're in the salon, can you be selfish?

Do you put your own needs in front of the people around you? Take a second to think about that.

2. How guilty are you of having favourites amongst your staff?

Are you someone that shows favouritism between different members of your team? And it's honesty time, just ask yourself that question.

3. How guilty are you of talking about people behind their backs?

Let's say a team member makes a habit of ringing in sick, do you go into the staff room and moan about it to other members of staff?

4. How guilty are you of making promises to your staff that you don't keep?

Some employers are very guilty of just saying what they need to say to get over a problem and then they forget about the promises they made.

5. How guilty are you of being intolerant, impatient or holding grudges?

You might think it's ok if you can be a bit grumpy, or sometimes hold a grudge against people who don't care about you, or do what you want ... but is it really ok?

6. Are you judgemental?

Do you go around judging people against your own standards whatever they may be? Or are your fairly open minded and tolerant and accept that there are different schools of thought?

7. Are you guilty of bullying in any form?

There are some employers who get what they want by hectoring, haranguing, nagging and telling people what to do all the time. And they do it in a negative way. Get real, this is bullying!

8. Are you guilty of blaming others rather than sharing or taking responsibility?

Some salon owners think that when things go wrong because mistakes are being made, it's only natural to make sure others take the blame. They believe they'll look weak or incompetent if they don't.

9. Are you guilty of being inconsistent or unfair with praise and discipline?

We tend to take our good staff for granted. They're generating a lot of turnover for us, with a positive attitude and causing no problems, so we just let them get on with it and assume they know how we feel about them. Instead we focus our attention on our problem people.

Big mistake!

Why?

Because what you focus on ... you get more of! Is that what you really want ... **more problem people?**

10. How guilty are you of having no measurement or feedback?

In other words, do your team know what's expected of them in terms of figures and production and do they know how they are performing relative to that expectation?

11. How guilty are you of not trusting?

Do you expect the worst from your staff or do you expect the best?

12. How guilty are you of not consulting or involving?

Do you just make the decisions and tell them ... this is how it's going to be? Or do you involve the team by getting their suggestions on how things can be improved or resolved?

13. How guilty are you of not listening?

Your team will be telling you things all the time, if you listen and as we saw in the last chapter, listening carefully to someone and proving it by repeating their words back to them in the form of a follow up question, is one of the most powerful trust building things you can do. **Listening is an essential part of your emotional 'Team Esteem' glue!**

How did you find the questions, I know I used to be guilty of quite a few! I'm sure you can see how your behaviour might have a massive effect on your ability to create **'Team Esteem'** and paying attention to getting it right is a vital part of the process.

3. "By only employing people whose contribution we can trust, respect and appreciate."

We can keep this one short and sweet. Use the selection process we went through together earlier in chapter 3 to weed out any new *Hyacinths* before they take root.

What you'll be left with is a team glued together by trust, respect and appreciation.

4. "By only employing people who can trust, respect and appreciate each other."

Let's imagine you've recruited well, you've **'managed'** the existing *Hyacinths* you had out of your salon and dealt with any personal bad habits that made it difficult for your staff to trust, respect and appreciate you.

Are you safe now ... can you relax?

You can ... sort of ... but **never** ever take the *Hyacinth* free status of your team for granted because it's highly likely at some point you'll notice your **'Team Esteem'** being tested by a change in the behaviour of one or more of your staff. If this happens it's your job to act ... quickly!

The behaviour of team members normally changes from being 'OK' to '*Hyacinth*' in reaction to changes in the behaviour of other people. As I mentioned in the last section it could be you causing the problem by falling back into your bad habits. If it's not that then usually it's a change in the family or social circumstances of the person concerned. I've seen problems caused when a team member:

- Meets an insecure new boyfriend/girlfriend who is desperate to take control of the relationship by splitting them from the group.

- Comes to the end of a long-term relationship which makes them question **'who they are'** and **'what their life is all about'.**

- Suddenly has to cope with parents who split up or divorce causing a massive change in the home environment which is then reflected at work.

- Suddenly has to cope with the bereavement or illness of someone close to them.

Don't be surprised if a massive change in a team member's life outside of work affects their behaviour inside work … but be prepared.

Be prepared to be supportive.

Be supportive, give them time to cope and/or recover, but **don't** let them off the hook. **They** are still responsible for their behaviour at work.

Do you remember in the chapter on **'You'** we said **we all have a choice about how we respond to things? Some respond by:**

- Becoming 'poor me' victims,

- Getting angry and taking that anger out on the people around them, either directly with confrontation or indirectly with gossip, backstabbing, manipulation, bullying or theft.

- Taking adversity on the chin and getting on with life.

Your team will normally respond incredibly well to a change or crisis in a member's life but if the new behaviour starts to cause damage to the team and their good will, you'll find the support and tolerance won't last forever and when it starts to run out, **you** have to manage the situation.

As much as you may want them to, your team won't do it for you … they'll self-destruct instead, **which is the last thing you want.**

I know that was a lot to take in but this step is so crucial you have to make sure you get it right, because this is where your team will either stand or fall.

The good news is if you get this part right consistently … **they'll take the next two steps quickly, easily and all by themselves!**

STEP 3 … EMOTIONAL ENGAGEMENT.

As you'll discover, when your team members feel emotionally secure, trusted, respected and appreciated they start to feel like they belong, feel like they matter, feel they're important. **In a nutshell they feel emotionally engaged.**

On **Step 1**, when it was **'just a job'** all you got for the salary you paid were their arms and legs.

No passion ... No commitment.

On **Step 2** everything started to change because you introduced the glue of emotional security, which means by the time you get them to **Step 3** and emotional engagement you're getting the passion and commitment of their hearts and minds thrown in for free.

Why free?

Because you pay them the same amount of money as **Step 1** employees, but they give you much better emotional value!

STEP 4 ... RESPONSIBILITY.

Get them to this stage – *and remember it happens automatically once you get them past Step 2* – and your team will take responsibility for their performance and when they do that ... **YOU DON'T HAVE TO!**

This means **'The Team Esteem Staircase'** is your route to freedom.

- Freedom to expand your business when you want to, just by expanding your team.

- Freedom to spend as much or as little time as you want in the salon.

- Freedom from worry about your staff and the problems you used to have.

<u>You</u> get the freedom because <u>they</u> are taking responsibility.

You also get to be a brilliant boss!

Think about it.

Very few salon owners are going to be working with their team in the same way that **you** are. The vast majority of your competitors will be getting **Step 2** wrong and this gives you a massive competitive advantage.

Why?

Because staff turnover costs you money and **'Team Esteem'** creates loyalty. Your staff will stay loyal because they know they can't get what you're giving them anywhere else. Keep on being a brilliant boss and you'll also find good staff from other salons will contact you to ask for a job.

Another important **'Team Esteem'** benefit is you don't have to spend most of your time **'managing'** your salon ... your **'responsible'** team will do it for you and they'll do it because they want to.

You need to understand that your job is to be the referee, the conductor or cheerleader for your team ... BUT and it's a **BIG BUT**; just like the referee doesn't play in the game and the conductor doesn't play in the orchestra ... you are **not** to be a member of your team. You are friendly, you are professional ... **but you absolutely must be separate from your team.**

Why is this important?

Because if you're the boss AND part of the team, it doesn't matter how well you delegate responsibilities, they'll delegate them back to you in the end ... because you're the top dog in the team, it all comes back to you. **It's just what happens, believe me I know!**

Your role is to provide the direction, the environment, the rules and the equipment they need so **they** can manage **themselves** effectively. Do it right and the good news is self-managing people are a joy to work with. They take responsibility, they come up with ideas for making things better, you'll find you can delegate to them and they just get on with it.

It's what allowed me to have the salon of my dreams, a salon that is successful whether I am there or not.

We've looked at **You** and **Your Team** and how they fit into giving you the salon of your dreams. There is one other 'people' part we need to look at ... **Your Clients!**

Chapter 7

Your Clients

Your clients also play a huge role in your success don't they, but they can also be the cause of some of your stress!

We've put in so much work up until this point.

- We've **got the right team.**

- We've **created systems** so that our **client journey/ experience** is delivered **consistently.**

- We've worked on ourselves to understand our behaviour and how to stop our **limiting beliefs** from **sabotaging** our dreams.

We're almost there with our **dream salon,** now we want to fill it with our **dream clients!**

We all have some don't we. Those clients who when you see their name in your column you smile.

You can't wait to see them, you enjoy doing their treatments, they're **on time,** and they **listen** to your recommendations, **purchase** products and visit often.

They're the people who **recommend** you to their friends, **support** your business and genuinely want to see you succeed!

Then there are the others.

You know who I mean. The ones who fill your stomach with dread when you see they've booked in.

Are they going to **show up** this time, if they do show up how **late** will they be?

Are they going to complain about prices going up?

Are they going to **cancel** last minute because they don't really **respect** you and what you do for them?

We all have some of these clients don't we!

What if I told you that about **80%** of your profits come from only **20%** of your clients ... which clients do you think would be in the 20%?

The ones who you enjoy spending time with, that support you and appreciate what you do for them?

Or the ones who complain, cancel and make your job more difficult?

The answer is quite obvious isn't it?

We'll look at profits in a lot more detail in the next chapter but what I want to focus on first is how we can make sure we have a salon full of 'loyal fans' who want to do business with you, will pay the prices you set out without blinking an eye and will appreciate you and your salon.

Let's go back to the **'Team Esteem Staircase'** we looked at in the last chapter, it was all about building trust within your team and creating lasting relationships.

Well we can do the same thing with our clients, we can create **'The Loyal Fan Staircase'** to build trust and define your relationship with your clients.

Just like before; if you create the right environment and *train your team to behave in the right way,* your clients will climb all the way to the top step of their staircase and become loyal fans of your business as part of a natural process ... **they won't be able to help themselves.**

Let's look at the steps.

Step 1 ... It's just a treatment

For clients on Step 1 coming to your salon is just a transaction.

Unconsciously the client thinks, *"I need a facial or some waxing. You're open, you're convenient, you have an appointment, your prices are OK ... you'll do."* This client may come once, they may come a dozen times, but at some point 'life' in the form of a better offer, or something more convenient, or simply a comment from a friend will break the pattern and they'll be gone; just because there was no emotional glue to hold them.

Step 2 ... Build rapport

If you ever want a client to move on to Step 2 of the staircase, you have to build rapport.

You have rapport when a client feels you '**know**' them, '**like/ respect**' them and '**trust**' them.

Like '**The Team Esteem Staircase**' this is where the emotional glue is applied to your relationship with clients and again this step is the danger zone.

Get it right and your team members will rapidly build a loyal army of happy clients … get it wrong and you'll always be relying on 'special offers' and finding new clients to stay in business.

There are two secrets to building rapport.

1. **People like people who 'like' them.** The question is … how do you show a client that you like them? It's easy when you know how.

- **Smile genuinely.** When you make eye contact with every client and smile, you'll see them smile back.

- **Give sincere compliments.** Stop focussing on yourself and pay every client a couple of sincere compliments. It shows you care.

- **Use your client's name.** Find out what they like to be called and once you know it, put a reminder in your computer, so you don't forget, and then use it regularly during their appointment.

- **Make regular eye contact.** Make sure you look directly into your client's eyes when they talk to you. This will show them you're interested.

- **Use humour.** It's OK to be playful and get silly sometimes. Don't be afraid to laugh, it's infectious.

- **Remember their preferred drink, their favourite nail colour.** This sort of thing matters and again it's just a case of making a note on your computer.

- **Remember what they tell you.** Clients will often tell you about the major events happening in their lives. Again, make a note on the computer and remind yourself before they come in. This is one of the most powerful things you can do to show a client you like them and they matter to you.

- **Never argue with a client.** You can never ever win in the long run, even if the client is wrong! Remember this isn't a game and we're not fighting a war either, we're running a business.

- **It there's a problem, keep calm.** Don't get dragged into the drama or emotional tension a problem can create.

- **Fix the experience.** Remember, if a client is unhappy it's not enough to fix the problem, you have to fix the experience. It's how they feel afterwards that matters.

2. People like people who are 'like' them.

The secret to this lies in the lessons we learned on *'reflective listening'* in the chapter on recruitment. *Reflective listening* makes building rapport with clients incredibly easy.

Here's a reminder of the basics.

- When you meet your client at the beginning of an appointment you'll start talking to them about how they are, what's happening at the moment, what they are looking for today and so on.

- Where possible without looking silly simply **copy their body language for a minute or two.** Remember; you take the time to do this because it makes them feel comfortable and as your conversation or consultation moves on make sure you watch for:

- A change of expression on their face; **they may smile, raise an eyebrow, blush or go pale.**

- A change of posture; **they may sit back, sit forward, lean towards or lean away from you, cross or uncross their arms or legs.**

- A gesture with their hands; **they may point at something imaginary, sit on their hands, make a chopping or pushing gesture. They may wave their hands about, touch their face or scratch their head.**

- All these changes can be a sign of **'emotion'** and that's what you're after, because you're looking for what matters to **them.**

- Now remember, once you spot it, you must reflect what you've seen back at them in a follow up question, to help you find out more about the **'emotion.'** Make sure you reflect the **same** word(s) and gesture(s) back to them when you ask your question.

For example, they might say *"My skin feels tight and dry at the moment."* *(As they say the words 'tight and dry' they might put their hands to their face and pull their skin tight.)* You could turn their reaction into a question like: *"I can see it really bothers you that your skin's feeling 'tight and dry"* *(and as you say the words 'tight and dry' you put your hands to your face and pull your skin tight)* would you like me to do something about it?

Remember, you're repeating part of what they said, in the same way they said it, but you've turned it into the form of a question.

Reflecting language and gestures back to a client gives them the feeling you understand them deeply and rapport will follow quite naturally.

Again it may feel a bit strange at first so practice on family and friends. Since incorporating this technique into our consultations we have seen our client relationships grow much faster. Clients trust you more and this makes them more likely to listen to your treatment and product recommendations.

Step 3 ... Don't take them for granted

Let's assume you've built good rapport and your client now feels emotionally glued to your salon. What comes next?

Simple ... you carry on making them feel special. You keep building rapport by doing everything that worked for **step 2**. You make sure you never take them for granted and occasionally you add some **'surprise and delight.'**

A free gift here, an invitation to a special event there, every little helps.

It pays to remember their birthdays, in fact it pays to be there to offer emotional support whenever something major happens in their life, such as:

- Births
- Deaths
- Weddings
- Divorces

You really can play a part in all these major events if you're sensitive enough … and clients will often remember when you do, so don't be surprised if it takes your relationship to the next level.

There's one extremely powerful reason why you'd take the time and trouble to do all this and it's because … **this is the step when loyal fans are created and they don't happen by accident.**

The fact is, if you have a real emotional connection with a client, but you don't deliver step 3 consistently they'll probably stay loyal to you **for a while** but they won't recommend you … **just in case you make them look silly in front of their friends.**

IMPORTANT POINT

Inconsistency can lose you clients very easily - the lesson here is that is can also cost you a lot of new clients, because nothing dries the word of mouth tap up more quickly than inconsistency!

By the way, a lot of salon owners think that simply having a *'recommend a friend'* scheme is all they need to attract 'word of mouth' clients but the fact is most of them are a waste of time in most salons.

Recommend a friend schemes **only** work when you provide a service worth recommending! They **only** work when you understand the power of **'The Loyal Fan Staircase'** simply because *'like attracts like'* and if your clients aren't on step 3 or 4 all you'll get are transactions, instead of relationships.

Step 4 ... Loyal fans

This is the final step and in a way it's the easiest to follow.

Every time a client recommends someone, make sure your computer system flags it up to you, so you can say thank you.

Then all you have to do is let the client who did the recommending know how their friend or family member is getting on from time to time.

It doesn't have to be a long-winded report, just a few words every now and then to remind them you didn't take their recommendation for granted and you haven't forgotten!

What sort of an impact do you think it would have on your business if you had a salon full of loyal fans? What would it look like for you, for your team?

We've taken a look at how we progress clients up **'The Loyal Fan Staircase',** now let's take a look at what and how you can communicate with your clients to help them climb your staircase.

One of the first points to consider is 'what' you are communicating to your clients. The secret to attracting new clients and turning enough of them into 'big spenders' is understanding and using a more 'joined up' form of marketing. When you get it right, you'll find that your loyal fans will spread the word for you by word of mouth; **the oldest, cheapest, and most effective marketing there is!**

You learned the formula for doing this in the recruiting chapter.

Do you remember **A.I.D.A.** ... Attention, Interest, Desire, Action?

Attention: Come up with a powerful headline, to grab the attention in a way that makes the reader recognise themselves, their problem or their desire.

Interest: Generate interest by showing your reader you understand them and have an answer to their problem/wish.

Desire: Build the desire by showing your reader what life will be like if they use your solution ... **but they need to act quickly because the opportunity is limited.**

Action: Tell them <u>exactly</u> what they've got to do to get what they want ... **and remind them to act quickly because the opportunity is limited.**

This formula is great. It gives you a step by step structure for writing effective adverts, texts, emails and content for Facebook, plus your website and newsletter.

You also need to make sure that all your marketing material is 'client focussed' rather than 'salon focussed' because unconsciously all any of us really think about when we're 'exposed' to marketing is … **What's in it for Me?**

Salon focussed marketing material says things like:

- We've been in business for 10 years.

- Our team is well trained.

- We only use top quality products.

Client focussed marketing says things like:

- You're going to love the fact that we've been in business for 10 years, because it means you're in experienced hands and we know how to take care of you!

- You can relax, safe in the knowledge that our team is well trained in the art of giving you exactly what you want.

- You're only human aren't you, and it's human to want the best … we agree! That's why we'll only ever use the best products on your skin.

Can you see, the same facts were presented with a **different** focus and it's a powerful difference, isn't it?

These are very powerful tools indeed but if your marketing is *'just another offer'*, if it's *'part of the noise'* if it's *'generic',* *'bland',* *'vanilla'* … you'll **always** struggle to attract people for any reason other than low, low prices and we know the problems that can cause.

Your salon might be **'convenient'**, you might be **'friendly'**, you might be **'nice'**, you might offer **'value'** – but so do a lot of other salons and you need to stand out … **you have to create salon marketing, that <u>dares</u> to be more!**

You have to create salon marketing … THAT DARES TO BE DIFFERENT!

What we really need to find is a simple process that any salon owner can use to create a marketing message *they* can deliver comfortably and consistently in a **'joined up'** way. It needs to be simple, but at the same time the message should be powerful enough to make them **'Stand out from the crowd.'**

When I first started working on this for my salon I asked myself the following question:

"Why should clients choose my salon rather than any of my competitors?"

It's a lot harder than you think! At first I gave the answers most salon owners give … *"Because we're friendly, we're good at what we do, we're well trained"* All important things but they didn't really make us stand out from the crowd. I got the team involved and we didn't really come up with anything much better.

So I asked our clients the question … *"What makes us different?"*

Now I was pleased to hear that all of the reasons we had come up with were on their lists too but then something happened which I didn't expect.

Clients comments said **"they feel we listen, understand and actually care about them".**

Now this information was marketing gold yet we didn't realise its importance because it was just something we did every day, naturally.

It allowed us to create a **'Unique Perceived Benefit'.**

This is simply an attractive marketing **'promise'** that you're happy you can deliver consistently ... **which you back up with a guarantee.** Now occasionally, when you look at what you do, you'll find the marketing 'promise' you can make to your clients is obvious, but in most cases you'll need to **'create'** it from scratch like we did.

The most successful 'Unique Perceived Benefit' there's ever been has to belong to Domino's Pizza.

Fresh Hot Pizza Delivered To Your Door, In 30 Minutes Or Less, Or It's Free!

Tom Monahan of Domino's Pizza created one of the most successful fast-food franchises of all time, using this; but what makes it so good?

Well; it simply promises his customers exactly what they **really** want and gives them a **guarantee** they'll get it.

They want it hot, they want it quickly and he guarantees to deliver in 30 minutes or it's FREE

That's what your 'Unique Perceived Benefit' needs to do; promise a result your clients really want ... **and guarantee they get it!**

So what result could you promise?

Well, promises based on something specific and measurable like saving time, saving money or getting something extra for nothing work well. There are many possibilities, but it's important that **whatever** you come up with reflects who you are.

Only then will you be able to deliver on your promise consistently.

As a team we brainstormed what we could do with the information our clients had given us about being listened to and feeling cared about.

We'd learnt that this was important to our clients and were confident that potential clients would also find this important.

It became our promise:

"Our Clients Know They Can Trust Us To Listen And Care, Because Of Our 100% 'Absolute Happiness' Guarantee. Now You Know, You Can Trust Us, To Look After You Too"

IMPORTANT POINT

REMEMBER your guarantee ... it's the bit that makes the promise special, it's the bit that makes you stand out from the crowd.

What should you give as a guarantee?

That's up to you and how confident you are of delivering.

We discussed this as a team and although they had reservations at first, because they thought, like many people do, that others would take advantage.

To give them a different perspective I asked the team if they would feel pleased if a client left our salon without feeling absolutely happy with their experience. Suddenly they could see what the guarantee meant in a different way.

I then asked them if they were confident they could deliver such a guarantee and what would our standards have to look like for this to happen consistently?

In other words I was asking if we could we live up to what we were promising?

We decided this was the way we wanted to go and our promise and guarantee was created.

We then went about spreading the message to all our clients. Look and you'll see that it's prominently placed on the homepage of our website, it's in our literature and even on the walls in the salon!

Everybody on the team understands that our job is to keep that promise ... **and if we don't, to happily pay up under our guarantee.**

By the way, this brings us to an important point. If you do have to pay up under your guarantee, don't be shy about it ... **publicise the fact.**

It might sound odd but letting clients know that if you do make a mistake you're happy to pay up under the terms of your guarantee, builds trust very quickly … **because it proves you practice what you preach!**

Having a guarantee is a real benefit to you because it:

- Makes your whole team work diligently to raise your standards by giving you a reputation to live up to.

- Gives you valuable feedback about problems, because more clients will <u>bother</u> to tell you if they're not happy: **Most unhappy clients usually just go home and tell everyone else, which is not what you want!**

- Encourages far more **'new'** clients to come in and give you a try because your guarantee will give them confidence.

So please get past the thing that worries most salon owners when I suggest they use a guarantee … **which is the fear that clients will rip them off.**

All of the research shows very few actually do. It means if you've got the guts to offer one you'll stand out from the crowd and attract lots of new clients.

It's not just research either. In the years since we implemented our promise and guarantee we've only had to pay up on it a couple of times. And because our guarantee is **'Absolute Happiness'** we did what was needed to make those clients happy.

And guess what, they are now loyal fans so it was a win for all concerned!

Chapter 8

Your Profit

It's time to talk numbers, and if you're anything like most salon owners and me it's probably your least favourite part of business.

Maybe subconsciously that's why it's one of the last chapters of this book!

I understand that the financial side of the business isn't a strength for most salon owners. But here's the problem ... **if we don't understand our numbers then most of us will end up doing far too much work for far too little reward.**

Remember, your salon has to make a healthy profit if it's going to give you everything you want.

I'll readily admit that I'm not an accountant and I don't claim to know everything there is about the financial side of your business either.

Instead I am a salon owner just like you, who eventually realised that if I really wanted to make my salon work for me I had to get to grips with the numbers.

So I did ... and if I managed it, there's no reason why you can't too!

This is why I want to help you in this chapter. I'm going to share with you some important basic concepts which, if you apply them consistently … **will ensure all of your hard work pays off and pays you better as well!**

Let's start with a question … **what is your current operating profit margin?**

Most salon owners don't know because profit's not something we set our businesses up to measure. This also means we don't plan for it or set it as a goal.

Instead we believe that getting busier and busier is the answer … **but if you're busy giving your profit away, it's obviously not the BEST answer!**

As a coach I've now worked with salon's that were fully booked 6 days a week but not making money … and couldn't understand why!

The solution to this problem is actually deceptively simple. Their costs were out of control which meant that even though they had lots of turnover and were working hard … **they didn't have the profit margin to pay for it.**

Let me introduce you to a simple idea, some of you may have come across it before, that has the power to transform any salon's ability to make a profit, by working smarter.

It's called the *80/20 rule* … or the **Pareto principle**, which says, that for many events, roughly **80%** of the effects will come from **20%** of the causes.

Put like that, it doesn't sound much does it, so you may be wondering ... **why is it a simple idea that has the power to transform any salon's ability to make a profit?**

It's actually an easy question to answer, because when it comes to your salon it means:

- **80%** of your profits are probably coming from just **20%** of the treatments on your price list.

- **80%** of your profits are probably coming from just **20%** of your clients.

- **80%** of your profits are probably coming from just **20%** of your staff.

This means if you are able to identify:

- Your profitable treatments.

- Your profitable clients.

- Your profitable staff.

You can change many things:

- You can change the treatments on your price list to focus on those that make the most profit.

- You can change the price you charge for things.

- You can change the products you choose to promote and market.

- You can change how you treat and reward your clients.

- You can change how you treat and reward your staff.

If you focus on the profitable **20%** of **everything** you and your team do … the effect on your profit **margin** will be amazing. The good news is, the profitable **20%** of everything is in your salon computer system, your salon price list and in your accounts and I'll show you what to look for.

Now do you remember I said … 80% of your profits will probably come from just 20% of the treatments on your price list?

Well it's true and it happens because very few salon owners create their price list with profit in mind *(I used to be one of those salon owners … but not anymore!)*

Instead they look at their competitors' prices and work around that, don't they?

This is a very dangerous thing to do because without realising, you can create a price list full of **'Profit Vampires'** and just as vampires only come out at night you won't even see them eating up your profits and sucking the life blood out of your business!

I love this term **'Profit Vampire'** and found it really helped me to understand my treatment menu, because like many of you I had just looked around at the competition to create my own when I first opened the salon. I hadn't really given it much thought since then apart from the odd price increase … but we all need to.

Profit Vampires do exist and to prove it I'm looking at the waxing section of a real beauty salon price list right now and using a simple formula, I can see something which should scare all of us!

Let me show you why. If the salon owner who created this had two beauty therapists, both fully booked waxing clients for a 39 hour week you'd presume they'd each take roughly the same amount of money, wouldn't you?

If one was doing 'Brazilians' and the other doing 'Underarm' waxing ... you'd presume wrong!

Based on this real price list:

- The Underarm waxing therapist would take ... £780.00

- The Brazilian waxing therapist would take... £1950.00

That's a difference in turnover of £1170 and a difference in profit of about £900 working the same hours, doing very similar work and that £900 is being eaten by the Profit Vampires ... **OUCH!!!!!**

Now let me emphasise this point, I can count on the fingers of one hand the number of salon price lists I've looked at which haven't been infested with profit vampires ...this is why the 80/20 rule is so powerful!

OK. I promised to explain the simple formula you can use to check for profit vampires ... it's called the **Pence Per Minute Formula**. This is what you need to do.

Get a copy of your treatment menu.

Next to the price of every service on it I want you to write the number of minutes you **book out for the treatment.**

Finally get a calculator and go down dividing the cost of every service by the number of minutes you book out and write the pence per minute next to each price. Just to be clear the formula is:

Price ÷ Minutes Booked out = Pence Per Minute Charged

To make it even clearer, here are the pence per minute calculations for the example I gave you a few moments ago.

Underarm wax   *£10 ÷ 30 mins = 33 pence per minute*

Brazilian wax   *£25 ÷ 30 mins = 83 pence per minute*

By the way, when we're talking in **'pence'** and **'minutes'** the differences don't sound a lot, do they. A few pence here, a few minutes there, as long as we're busy ... *so what!*

IMPORTANT POINT!

You need to make sure you've learned the 'so what' lesson. When you have busy staff doing the wrong things on your price list, for hours, days or weeks at a time ... the difference can turn out to be extremely damaging because of the Profit Vampires!

You're probably thinking; that's fine as far as it goes Kelly, I understand what you're saying, but how do I know where to set my pence per minute to avoid the profit vampires?

Here's a simple formula to help you calculate the **minimum** pence per minute figure you should allow on your pricelist. I stress minimum because there is **no maximum** ... if the market will stand it, you should charge it and I'll explain why in a minute.

Here's the formula:

- Take your target turnover for the year.

- Divide it by 39 weeks (using 39 weeks instead of 52 weeks, allows for holidays and quiet days/times because your salon will **never** be fully staffed or fully booked every day)

- Divide the answer by the number of hours a full time therapist works for you.

- Divide the answer by the number of full time therapists you have. (if you have part timers, add up all their hours and divide the answer by the number of hours **one** full timer does then add the answer you get to your full time total)

- Divide the answer by 60 (minutes in an hour)

And the final answer you get will be your minimum **pence per minute. Base your price list on that as a minimum, keep reasonably busy and your salon will hit your target ... guaranteed!**

Let me give you an example of how this formula would apply to a typical medium sized salon.

Let's assume we're looking at an annual target of £300,000 with **3 full time therapists** working **40 hours a week** and **3 part timers doing 25hrs, 24hrs, and 21hrs.** (Added together the part time hours = **70.** Divide **70** by the **40hrs** the full timers do and your 3 part timers do the equivalent hours of **1.75** full timers. So your final total of full timers would be **3 + 1.75 = 4.75**)

Now with all the answers rounded up or down to the nearest full pence as you go along, the calculation would look like this.

		Your Salon
£300,000 annual target ÷ **39 weeks**	= £7692.31	
£7692.31 ÷ **40hrs a week**	= £192.31	
£192.31 ÷ 4.75 **full time therapists**	= £40.49	
£40.49 ÷ **60 mins**	= 67 pence per minute	

I promised to explain why this figure should only be a minimum and you should charge more where you can, didn't I?

Well, the reason is every time you advertise, it costs you money. Every time you offer a discount, it costs you money. Every time you give away a FREE service or gift … **it costs you money!**

If you focus your special offers on the items with lots of extra built in profit, because their pence per minute is well above your minimum, you can afford to run offers because you will have the built in extra profit margin to do it.

Easy when you know how, right?

Also it will pay you to become a salon that '**specialises in**' and becomes '**recognised as an expert**' in the services with a high profit margin.

When you do that successfully you'll find your profits go through the roof because of the '**low cost**' and '**no cost**' benefits of '**word of mouth**' marketing.

In other words become an expert or specialist in the high profit services and you won't even have to spend some of the profit on attracting and keeping new clients … **your 'word of mouth' reputation will do it for you!**

Now, when I share the '**pence per minute**' formula with salon owners, there's a question that always comes up, and it's this. "When I've worked out my minimum price for (then they name a treatment) it comes to (then they name the price) … **which is more than my clients will pay.**"

There are 3 answers to this question.

- **That's not a problem.** The higher price will choke off a lot of demand but the few you still do will be so much more profitable you won't lose out.

- **Keep prices close to where they are and allow less time instead.** As you've probably worked out by now ... 'time is money.' You'd be amazed how much the pence per minute you can earn shoots up when you shave 5 or 10 minutes off the time allowed to do a treatment.

- **Do nothing.** If you take this option you need to realise it's probably a sign of low self-esteem and limiting beliefs; but if you insist on doing nothing, at least make sure this is a service you **NEVER EVER** discount ... **all that does is make a bad situation worse!**

So now we understand how the 80/20 rule applies to our price list, the next question has to be ... how does it apply to our clients?

Do you remember we said that 80% of our profits would probably come from 20% of our clients? Well it's true and for proof you'll find the best place to look, is on your salon computer system. By the way I'm often asked which system I use and whether I'd recommend it, or not.

I use the Phorest salon software system. In my experience the system is brilliant for online booking, salon marketing and reports. The training is excellent and so is the support.

Phorest is the 4th system I've used so I have had a few to compare it to ... **and yes I would definitely recommend it! You can find out more if you're interested at www.phorest.com**

Anyway, back to our profitable clients.

I'd start by selecting a list of your top 500 clients; by spend, for the last year. When you look at it you'll probably see the typical salon pattern, which consists of a group of clients at the top who are your '**Big**' spenders.

Next you should be able to identify a larger group of '**Typical**' spenders.

Finally you'll see the largest group of all, as your client spending figures dribble slowly downwards in ever decreasing amounts to form your '**Small**' spenders (you want to avoid them if at all possible).

Why avoid them?

IMPORTANT POINT

Because they'll take 80% of your time and only give you 20% of your profits!

Bearing that in mind, the important question is ... should you treat all of your clients the same, or should your '**Big**' spenders be recognised and rewarded in some way?

I don't know what your answer will be ... but I **do** know what it **should** be!

Of course you should make a fuss of and recognise your best customers. Give them flowers from time to time, hold an annual party for them, or take them out to dinner. Invite them to focus groups and listen to what they have to say. Give them a proper V.I.P club to belong to ... **Do whatever it takes.**

Why?

Because you're far less likely to lose them if you show you appreciate them, aren't you? Remember, they are bringing you the majority of your profits!

There's another benefit as well. If you make a fuss publicly, other clients will know what you're doing and some of them will be attracted to join in and the only way they can do that ... is to spend more, which is **exactly** what you want.

To sum it up, following the '**make a bigger fuss of your best clients**' policy achieves three things:

1. Your '**Big**' spenders stay loyal for longer.

2. Your '**Typical**' spenders aspire to join the big spender group.

3. Your '**Small**' spenders either get more involved or go away and eat up someone else's profits.

Whatever happens ... your profits go up.

The final piece of the 80/20 profit jigsaw was that **80% of your profits will probably come from 20% of your staff.** Again it's very likely to be true and there's another simple formula that will help you identify who the '**good guys**' are, because as you'll see more clearly later in the chapter ... **you can't afford to be carrying passengers.**

The formula you should apply to all of your productive staff is this:

Turnover divided by Hours Worked (deduct holiday/time off sick/unpaid leave etc) **divided by their hourly target** (4 times their basic hourly rate is widely used) ... **then press the % key ... which will give you their % performance against target.**

So let's assume you have a therapist who has taken £5000 in a month, *(by the way I'm using a month as an example ... the formula works just as well over a day, a week, a month, or even a year)* worked **180** hours and their hourly target is **£40** (£10 per hour basic pay x 4 = £40 per hour target)

The sum would look like this.

£5000 turnover ÷ **180** hours worked ÷ **£40** then press the % key and the answer is **69.44%**

Which means; they only reached **69.44%** of their months target and are probably costing you money!

Now applying the formula to one person is only the beginning ... I go further ... much further. I want my **whole** team to **average** 100% and for that to happen the experienced ones have to be averaging comfortably **over** 100%, because any new or recently qualified people will inevitably be below target while they are building and they'll be dragging the team average down.

By the way there's a massive difference between someone at **69.44%** who's actively growing their turnover and will soon reach target and someone who's stuck at that level and not making progress.

The way you'd work with each one would be very different.

The 'grower' will respond to **'towards'** motivation because they can see what they are aiming for, believe they can do it and they want to get there. For them encouragement and rewards will work well.

The 'sticker' by contrast is someone who has reached their natural level and if you leave them alone, that's where they'll stay. Plodding along; costing you money. **More fool you if you accept that situation, or believe there's nothing you can do about it.**

These people need **'away'** motivation. You need to turn the comfort zone where they are living into a 'discomfort zone' by having regular meetings and explaining in a calm non-judgemental language that their current level of performance is below the standards required and if it continues ... **their employment won't!**

Be fair. Give them an achievable goal and a reasonable amount of time to reach it. Measure their progress with weekly meetings if needed. Praise progress but be prepared to make the decision to end their employment if they don't reach the target by the deadline ... **don't make the mistake many salon owners make of letting things drift.**

The process I've just described is, as far as I'm aware, legal in the UK as long as you are clear, consistent and fair with your staff.

By the way I'm not a lawyer so I don't **'do'** legal advice.

If I were you though, I'd belong to an organisation like the **Federation of Small Businesses** or the **National Hairdressers**

and Beauty Federation both of which provide free legal advice and indemnity as part of their membership package.

As a member ... whenever you have a problem you can make a quick phone call before following **exact** instructions you're given. Do this and should the problem end up '**going legal**' further down the line, you're covered.

The truth is I could write a whole other book on the **80/20** rule and still not cover every application! It never surprises me that a new client's situation, although different from the last, can be helped using this rule. Just remember that every journey starts somewhere and the **80/20** rule is a very good way to start!

When I started looking at these three key areas in my salon the difference it made to my profits was huge. Be brave, step out of your comfort zone and ditch those treatments and clients that aren't working for you!

I was very apprehensive at first and thought we would lose clients, which we did, but **only** the ones who weren't good for our salon profits.

By focusing on the treatments and clients that were good for the salon it meant productivity in the team also went up. As the team were now doing treatments they enjoyed on clients they wanted to work with and they were being rewarded well for doing so.

Now, so far we've looked at improving productivity by working smarter using the 80/20 rule as a guide, but there's another important part of the puzzle and that's to ... **ruthlessly control your costs by demanding and expecting Value For Money for every penny you spend.**

Why?

Because every pound you save, is yours. You've got the lot. No costs. No tax. No wages. No stock ... **NOTHING ... it's all <u>extra</u> profit.**

On the other hand ... every pound of additional turnover you generate is **riddled with costs**, which means very little of it is profit.

This means the fastest, most effective way to recover lost profits is <u>always</u> going to be by getting maximum value for every penny you spend.

Getting value for money is the name of the game, but we have to do it in a way that's sensitive to our client's expectations and respects the prices we charge.

If we're going to control our costs and get value for money, we need to be planning and measuring our spending and the best way to do that is by budgeting ... **which isn't something that comes naturally to most salon owners, is it?**

It definitely didn't come naturally to me, which is why I'm going to keep this simple.

For example, contrary to what most accountants do, I always work with VAT <u>inclusive</u> figures when I'm budgeting.

Think about it.

When you pay your suppliers **VAT is included**, isn't it? When you pay **HM Revenue and Customs** your VAT once a quarter you're paying out of your bank account aren't you? This means, in my non accounting opinion, it's far easier to budget for and measure what's **actually** going in and out of your account, rather than trying to make sense of **'adjusted'** figures that don't match your bank statement.

It's also important, when we're budgeting to remember there are only 100 pence, or cents in the Pound, Euro or Dollar ... **No matter how many you wish there could be.**

This means we have to split every pound that we earn into 100 pence and then budget how many of those pence we can afford to spend on different items.

To keep it simple I break my 100 pence budget into the following groups and targets for my salon.

- **Profit** (My normal target is a 20% operating profit)

- **VAT** (In the UK the average real cost of VAT to your business after you've claimed back what you can is 13%)

- **Wages/NI** (My target is 40% including the owner's salary)

- **Stock** (My target is 14%)

- **Rent/Rates** (My target is 5%)

- **Sundries** (Everything else we need to run the business and my target is 8%)

By the way ... Did you notice that profit was at the top of the list?

It's there because it should be non-negotiable. To have a successful business we have to make a profit, which means we have to plan and budget for it ... **end of story!**

Going back to my groups and targets, did you also notice that **20%** profit and **13%** VAT add up to **33%** leaving me with **67%** to pay for everything else? It has to be like that.

The VAT **is** non-negotiable isn't it, and the profit as we've just seen **should** be non-negotiable which means, as much as we may want more ... until the chancellor cuts VAT ... **67 pence is all we've got.**

It might help to see my figures in a bar chart to make them clearer.

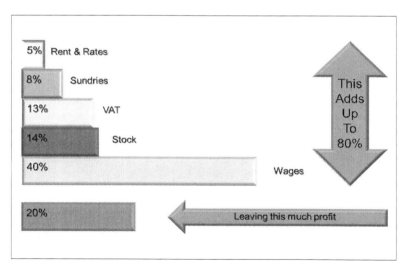

Sadly figures like these are not very common. Instead of making 20% operating profit the average salon struggles to make 5% after the owner has paid themselves properly, so why does this happen?

It happens because costs are not being measured and controlled as well as they should be and when they slip even just a little, it's amazing how quickly the profit picture can change.

Let me show you.

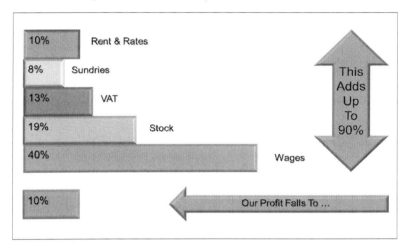

In this example a **5% overspend** on rent and rates and a **5% overspend** on stock has slashed the profit margin to **10%**, which doesn't sound too bad until you realise … **turnover would have to double to make the same amount of profit as before!**

Now, the sad fact is it's rare to see only some of the costs get out of control … **normally if the budget's going to slip it will slip on everything.**

So what does that picture look like when that happens?

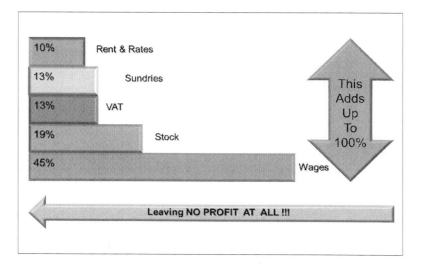

In this example the salon owner is only overspending by **5%** on the four target areas, which doesn't sound a lot but the fact is **4 x 5% = 20%** … which means their profit margin has gone completely and they are working for **NOTHING!**

So the lessons we can learn from these examples are simple.

- No matter what business you're in there are only 100 pence in the Pound.

- Decide how many pence are going to be profit and make it non-negotiable.

- Make sure you budget for the net cost of VAT as well.

- Whatever is left after profit and VAT are deducted is what you've got left to run your business. (67% is the target if 20% is your profit target)

- It doesn't really matter how you split up the 67% as long as your percentages add up to 67%. If they add up to more, it comes out of your profit, which as we've seen can rapidly shrink away to nothing!

In case you're wondering, here's an easy way to work out your percentages using a calculator. Take wages for example. You'll need your wages cost and your VAT inclusive turnover for the **same** period.

Now just enter your wages cost into the calculator and press ÷ next enter your total turnover figure and press % there's your answer!

So for example, if your wages were £87,000 and your turnover was £153,000 your calculation would look like this.

87,000 ÷ 153,000 then press % = 57%

There's one more thing we need to pay attention to, it's something that should be simple but many salon owners (and I include myself in that group) struggle with it.

What am I talking about?

MANAGING YOUR CASHFLOW!

Now, there's a saying I was introduced to which puts everything into perspective, in fact I was introduced to it at a seminar with a group of salon owners just like me.

"Turnover's vanity, profit is sanity and cash is king!"

We had to stand up, form a circle, hold hands and scream it at the top of our voices ... **5 times!**

As I'm sure you can imagine, this saying is embedded into my memory, and that's a good thing because it is that important.

I **need** to remember this because 'running out of cash' kills more salons than any other single reason.

In fact it's so important I want you to do the exercise too ... so make sure you're alone, - *we don't want anyone thinking you're going loopy, do we – and try it yourself.*

Try saying out loud ...

- *"Turnover's vanity, profit is sanity and cash is king!"*
- *"Turnover's vanity, profit is sanity and cash is king!"*
- *"Turnover's vanity, profit is sanity and cash is king!"*
- *"Turnover's vanity, profit is sanity and cash is king!"*
- *"Turnover's vanity, profit is sanity and cash is king!"*

So the lesson is ... **MAKE SURE YOU NEVER RUN OUT OF CASH!**

You're probably thinking, that sounds great Kelly ... but how?

Well start by having at least 3 bank accounts.

1. Your personal account.

2. Your business account.

3. Your high interest business savings account.

Next ... As an **absolute** rule keep your personal and business spending apart. It's a huge mistake to get them mixed up, because you never get a clear picture of what's yours and what isn't.

It's also a huge mistake to keep all of your business funds in one account because it lulls you into a false sense of security thinking things are OK, there's money in the bank ... **until your wages bill, your VAT bill, and your personal or corporation tax bill all become due within a few days and you haven't planned for it.**

Then suddenly you can be in trouble ... **BIG TROUBLE.**

Because of this it makes sense to take 33% of your turnover each week and put it in your high interest savings account and find a way to run your business with the rest.

Why 33%?

Do you remember earlier we said we want **20% profit** and **VAT costs you 13%?** Add the two together and you get **33%**, which leaves **67%**, which is the salon budget I suggested you aim to keep to.

If the **33%** is safe in another account you can pay your VAT bill when it comes ... **no problem!**

You can pay your personal or corporation tax bill when it comes, *(which you should pay out of your profits)* ... **no problem.**

If you find you have to keep dipping into your high interest savings account to pay other bills – like wages for example – you're getting an excellent early warning system that your profits are under attack and you need to do something about it!

The truth is, that when it comes to cash flow problems salon owners fall into two general groups.

For some, jumping from one cash flow crisis to the next is normal; it's just how they do things.

If this is you then sadly you deserve no sympathy, in fact you deserve every sleepless night you get. We're back to chapters one and two. **You** are responsible and managing your cash flow is something you can delegate if it's not one of your strengths!

The other group who have problems **don't** make a habit of it, they get caught out when they're not expecting it, normally because their costs go up and their profit margin goes down. Relying on your accountant and your annual accounts to sound the alarm that this happened is risky because by the time you realise ... **it's too late.**

That's why creating a separate high interest savings account which can give you a built-in early warning system is so useful.

I found this a great tool to flag up when profits were dropping below my target, and it still happens sometimes, but I am able to spot it quicker and put things in place to fix it.

OK, I think that's enough on formulas, profit, budgeting, cash flow and margins, don't you!

If you're anything like me your brain is probably fried by now ... **because we're not accountants, are we!**

Speaking of accountants, if you find yours isn't the most helpful, doesn't really understand your salon and only ever contacts you when their bill is due, I have great news! Did you know that there are accountants out there that specialise in our industry?

I work with Chris and his team at **CDC Accounting** and they really understand the salon industry, in fact Chris's wife actually owns one.

If you are looking for an accountant that will support you and help you to understand your numbers, then I highly recommend getting in touch with Chris's team. Working with them has really helped my salon and I am sure it would do the same for yours.

Anyway, at least we now know what happens when we work smart by:

- Employing the right people

- To provide the right treatments

- To the right clients

- With a budget that has 20% profit built in

- And we manage our cash flow properly

In other words ... **We know how to make our salon work, so we don't have to!**

You need to know there are many salons that have benefitted from these lessons ... **mine included!**

It's for that reason I'm so passionate about sharing them.

Chapter 9

So What's Next?

If I've inspired you to take action, then all the work put into creating it was worthwhile, because as I discovered after talking with a lovely salon owner from **Newcastle** who heard me speaking about **'Profit Vampires'** at an industry event ... I love helping salon owners change their lives.

She heard what I'd said and made the decision to ask me for help implementing the changes she knew she needed to make.

I said yes, we worked together, **her salon profits shot up**, and I discovered that I **loved** coaching salon owners to success.

With this in mind ask yourself if you're happy with your salon right now.

Is it giving you the life and lifestyle you want?

If your answer is yes that's great news, but if you'll allow me to be blunt with you for a moment ... you are in the minority!

If, however you're one of the majority who are **not** getting the life and lifestyle they want then you're obviously being deeply affected by some of the issues I've raised.

If this is true then you need to decide whether you're going to sort it out for yourself or ask for help like the salon owner from Newcastle.

It's an important decision, and before you take it you need to be aware some recent research has shown that:

- Learning about an idea in a book like this and thinking ... *"that's good"* the odds of you actually taking action and using it are **10%**

- If you take the idea and make a **decision** to try it, your chances of taking action improve to **25%**

- If you make a decision and set a deadline, your odds improve to 40%

- If you make a decision, set a **deadline** and come up with a plan to follow, they improve to **50%**

- If you make a decision, set a deadline and come up with a **written plan** to follow, they improve to **60%**

- If you make a decision, set a deadline, come up with a written plan to follow and then share it with someone you trust, like a **coach or mentor**, who will hold you to account ... your odds of being successful increase to **95%**

Knowing the simple fact that, *making a written plan and then sharing it with someone you trust, who'll hold you to account,* increases your odds of success dramatically!

It certainly worked for the salon owner from Newcastle and let's face it … Who wouldn't enjoy the fact that great results are **95% guaranteed!**

You're probably thinking … if I choose to join the 95% club and ask you to be my coach or mentor Kelly, it's probably going to cost me money … **but would you be right?**

YES & NO!

Yes: For your **own** good you'd have to pay. There's plenty of research to prove you wouldn't value the support and advice if it came for free … **Paying for it makes it powerful.**

No: Because the truth is your payments would be an investment. An investment that will probably pay for itself **10 times over** in improved profits, not to mention the priceless benefit of owning a salon that demands less time and less emotional energy to run.

What price would you put on peace of mind and getting your life back?

The really good news is I give an unconditional 90-day **"Total Happiness" Guarantee.**

What this means is that if **AT ANY TIME DURING THE FIRST 90 DAYS OF US WORKING TOGETHER** you decided that it wasn't what you were expecting or you couldn't see yourself getting the results you want … **you can change your mind.**

Simply let me know you want to stop and without any fuss or drama I promise I'll refund every penny or cent you've paid.

With a guarantee like that ... you really have got nothing to lose from giving coaching a try!

Just send an email to kelly_shaw@me.com telling me you want to join the 95% club and we can get started.

About The Author

Kelly Shaw has a strong passion for the Well-being and Spa Industry. With over 25 years experience at all levels of business, her dedication and drive has enabled her to achieve professional success as Spa Director for some of the world's most exclusive resorts in Thailand, Malaysia and the Caribbean, as well as Senior Educator for Dermalogica and the International Dermal Institute.

Founder of Hampshire's multi-award winning boutique salon k:SPA, Kelly's focus for the past 12 years has been to create her own unique style of Salon that creates a Spa experience. The magic formula is her team of k:SPA Ambassadors. By creating a positive and dynamic atmosphere based on motivation, training, knowledge sharing and inspiration, Kelly has proven success of k:SPA's continual growth by rewarding the exceptional performance by every member of the team with the experience of owning their own Salon together - a truly modern way of Salon Management.

Driven by a strong desire for continuous improvement, Kelly employs the best practices whilst maintaining an active interest in researching new industry techniques, treatments and technologies.

The reward of seeing her team flourish led to the desire to share her knowledge and help others succeed. Coaching and mentoring salon owners and managers has now naturally progressed into sharing her learnings further and the writing of this book

Acknowledgements

I'd like to thank my friends and family for all of their encouragement throughout this process.

I'd also like to thank the whole of the k:SPA team, both past and present, for working with me on the principles contained within this book. For teaching me lessons every day and for believing in me. If it wasn't for your continued support of my vision then none of this would have been possible.

I'd especially like to thank Simon for believing in me and encouraging me to take this step, even when my limiting beliefs tried to get in my way. For holding me accountable and supporting me throughout every step of this whole process.

Finally, I'd like to thank all of the industry professionals who have supported me in this journey, especially the salon owners I work with, you truly do inspire me every day.